STUDENT UNIT GUIDE

UNIT

3B

D1353915

Go
& Politics

Introducing Political Ideologies

Barry Pavier

Series Editor: Eric Magee

Philip Allan Updates, an imprint of Hodder Education, an Hachette UK company, Market Place, Deddington, Oxfordshire OX15 0SE

Orders

Bookpoint Ltd, 130 Milton Park, Abingdon, Oxfordshire OX14 4SB
tel: 01235 827720
fax: 01235 400454
e-mail: uk.orders@bookpoint.co.uk
Lines are open 9.00 a.m.–5.00 p.m., Monday to Saturday, with a 24-hour message answering service. You can also order through the Philip Allan Updates website: www.philipallan.co.uk

ISBN 978-0-340-98709-4

First printed 2009
Impression number 5 4 3 2
Year 2013 2012 2011 2010

This guide has been written specifically to support students preparing for the Edexcel A2 Government & Politics Unit 3 examination. The content has been neither approved nor endorsed by Edexcel and remains the sole responsibility of the author.

Typeset by Phoenix Photosetting, Chatham, Kent
Printed by MPG Books, Bodmin

Hachette UK's policy is to use papers that are natural, renewable and recyclable products and made from wood grown in sustainable forests. The logging and manufacturing processes are expected to conform to the environmental regulations of the country of origin.

Contents

Introduction

■ ■ ■

Content Guidance

■ ■ ■

Questions and Answers

Introduction

The Edexcel Advanced (A2) GCE in Government & Politics is a two-unit course. This guide to Unit 3B Introducing Political Ideologies has been written to help you prepare more effectively for the unit test. It provides an outline of the structure of the unit, guidance on all aspects of the content, exemplar questions and answers with examiner comments and advice on how the mark scheme works. Unit 4B Other Ideological Traditions is covered in a separate guide.

Unit 3B focuses on four ideologies: liberalism, conservatism, socialism and anarchism. For each ideology you need to know the core ideas, doctrines and theories as they affect views on human nature, the state, society and the economy.

In addition, you need to understand the differing views about and tensions within each ideology:
- in liberalism: classical liberalism vs modern liberalism
- in conservatism: traditional conservatism (including what is termed 'one-nation' conservatism) vs the 'New Right'
- in socialism: revolutionary socialism vs evolutionary socialism, and revisionist socialism vs fundamentalist socialism
- in anarchism: individualist versions vs collectivist versions of anarchism, and also anarchism's relationships with liberalism and socialism (you will also need to be aware of the attempts made by anarchists to translate their ideas into practice)

How to use this guide

The guide is divided into three sections:
- The **Introduction** sets out the aims of the guide, the details of the unit specification and the skills required for studying the unit and preparing for the unit test.
- The **Content Guidance** section explains the key concepts and issues in each part of the specification in detail. The coverage follows the outline of the specification.
- The **Questions and Answers** section contains a selection of questions that reflect the style of Unit 3B. There are sample answers of varying length and quality, each with a commentary indicating the strengths and weaknesses of the response to help you to understand precisely what examiners are looking for.

The unit at a glance

Each of the ideologies has to be studied in relation to a number of key concepts. These are ideas that are fundamental to the particular ideology. You need to know not only the definitions of each individual concept but also how they relate to each other and contribute to the ideology's attitude towards wider issues.

Liberalism

Key concepts	Content explanation
• Individualism • Freedom • Justice • Rationalism • Equality • Liberal democracy • Constitutionalism • Consent	• A knowledge of core ideas, doctrines and theories of liberal ideology, particularly as they affect liberal views on human nature, the state, society and the economy • An ability to discuss differing views and tensions within liberal ideology, notably between liberalism and modern liberalism

Conservatism

Key concepts	Content explanation
• Tradition • Organic society • Hierarchy • Authority • Property • Paternalism • Libertarianism • Authoritarianism • Neo-liberalism • Neo-conservatism	• A knowledge of core ideas, doctrines and theories of conservative ideology, particularly as they affect conservative views on human nature, the state, society and the economy • An ability to discuss differing views and tensions within conservative ideology, particularly related to the divisions between traditional conservatism and the 'New Right'

Socialism

Key concepts	Content explanation
• Cooperation • Fraternity • Collectivism • Social equality • Communism • Social democracy • Social justice • 'Third way'	• A knowledge of core ideas, doctrines and theories of socialist ideology, particularly as they affect socialist views on human nature, the state, society and the economy • An awareness of differences within socialism, in particular differences between revolutionary socialism and evolutionary socialism and between fundamentalist socialism and revisionist socialism (there will be no question set solely on twentieth-century communism)

Anarchism

Key concepts	Content explanation
• **Autonomy** • **Utopianism** • **Mutualism** • **Egoism** • **Anarcho-communism** • **Anarcho-capitalism** • **Anarcho-syndicalism**	• A knowledge of core ideas, doctrines and theories of anarchist political thought • An awareness of the breadth of anarchism, particularly of the differences between collectivist anarchism and individualist anarchism, and anarchism's relationship to socialism and liberalism • A knowledge of the difficulties anarchists have faced in translating their goals into successful political action

Each of these concepts is explained separately in the Content Guidance section. Their relationship to key issues is also dealt with there.

Examination skills

Your answers in the unit test will be marked according to three common assessment objectives. Each assessment objective is given a weighting. At A2, 50% is allocated to AO2 (analysis and evaluation), 30% to AO1 (knowledge and understanding) and 20% to AO3 (communication). This means that while you need to be able to demonstrate knowledge (AO1) and communicate your ideas clearly (AO3), most emphasis is placed on your ability to analyse and evaluate (AO2).

AO1	Demonstrate knowledge and understanding of relevant institutions, processes, political concepts, theories and debates	30%
AO2	Analyse and evaluate political information, arguments and explanations, and identify parallels, connections, similarities and differences between aspects of the political systems studied	50%
AO3	Construct and communicate coherent arguments making use of a range of appropriate political vocabulary	20%

Your Edexcel Unit 3 answers will be marked according to these assessment objectives. Remember that you will not just be given an overall mark out of 15 for each of your three short-answer questions and 45 for your essay question. In each answer, marks will be given for each assessment objective in the proportions shown above. The total for each question will be the sum of the separate marks for each of AO1, AO2 and AO3.

- Short-answer questions:
  AO1 = 5 marks
  AO2 = 7 marks
  AO3 = 3 marks
  Total = 15 marks

- Essay questions:
  AO1 = 12 marks
  AO2 = 24 marks (includes 12 marks for synopticity)
  AO3 = 9 marks
  Total = 45 marks

In order to get the best possible mark, you need to take a few essential steps:

- Understand the question. Focus on command words (e.g. analyse, evaluate, discuss, identify) and do what they say. Short-answer questions will be more focused on knowledge and understanding of key concepts. Essays require you to make a judgement, which is signaled by command words such as 'how far' and 'to what extent'.
- Answer all aspects of the question. If the question asks 'How and why...', you must give significant space to both of these (at least 30% to each).
- Use examples to support each point you make. As many as possible of these should be contemporary, which shows that you really understand the point you have made and have not simply memorised a list from a textbook. It is most effective when done in separate paragraphs.
- Use correct and precise political vocabulary. This is not only because 20% of the marks are specifically allocated for AO3. Correct terminology allows you to make points with clarity and precision. It saves you precious writing time in examinations and also makes your point absolutely clear to the examiner.

In addition to assessment objectives, there are performance descriptors for answers on the A/B and E/U grade boundaries. They give you a good idea of what is required to produce the sort of answer that will gain a top grade. You may find it useful to check your practice answers against these criteria, especially with relation to AO3, which is where many otherwise excellent answers frequently lose out. In fact, if you have written your answer so that you meet the A/B level requirements for AO3, it is likely that you will have met them for AO1 and AO2 as well.

Synopticity

In the essay questions, 12 of the 24 marks for AO2 are for 'synopticity'. Synopticity means learning to develop an all-round, integrated understanding of the subject.

Synoptic skills involve:

- the ability to identify alternative viewpoints or perspectives on an issue or question
- an awareness of the nature and extent of rivalry between these viewpoints
- an awareness of the significance of the viewpoints for an understanding of the issue or question

In this unit, synopticity will be achieved by demonstrating your ability to explain how political ideologies shape political argument and understanding. This can be done in two ways:

Grade	AO1	AO2	AO3
A/B boundary	Candidates characteristically: • demonstrate accurate, detailed and comprehensive knowledge of political institutions and processes, and a competent understanding of political concepts, theories and debates, incorporating the relevant specification content • produce answers that fully address the requirements of the question • demonstrate good contextual awareness • provide accurate evidence and, where appropriate, contemporary examples deployed to illustrate points made	Candidates characteristically: • provide analysis that synthesises political concepts, theories and issues • evaluate political information clearly and fully, using appropriate evidence that may be drawn from the whole specification • make effective comparisons, explaining parallels, connections, similarities and differences	Candidates characteristically: • construct and communicate cogent and coherent arguments and explanations • illustrate a clear sense of direction and, where appropriate, culminate in a coherent conclusion which flows from discussion • use a range of relevant and appropriate political vocabulary
E/U boundary	Candidates characteristically: • demonstrate an outline knowledge and understanding of political institutions and processes, political concepts, theories and debates, with evidence of some relevant specification content • make a limited attempt at answering the question • demonstrate some basic contextual awareness • provide some relevant evidence or examples	Candidates characteristically: • offer limited analysis that shows some awareness of differing ideas • attempt a simple evaluation of political institutions, processes, behaviour, arguments or explanations, and make some comparisons • outline basic concepts and theories • demonstrate some recognition of basic parallels and connections or similarities and differences	Candidates characteristically: • construct and communicate some arguments and explanations with a structure that is narrative or descriptive • illustrate a sense of direction and, where appropriate, offer a conclusion, though relationship with the preceding discussion may be tenuous or implicit • use some relevant evidence and some appropriate political vocabulary

- by understanding how the ideologies differ on crucial issues, such as society, human nature and the state
- by appreciating how there are fundamental differences within each ideology over central beliefs and values

To achieve this you will have to draw on your learning from the AS units. For instance, in Unit 1 you will have learned about the differences between the Labour and Conservative parties, and then the differences between 'old' and 'New' Labour and 'traditional conservatism' and the 'New Right'. You will need to use this knowledge and understanding to assist you in the study of socialism and conservatism.

In Unit 2, you learned about a number of topics such as constitutionalism, federalism, the fusion/separation of powers and civil liberties, which provide the basis for a study of liberalism and anarchism. This will constitute part of your study for the A2 units and a starting point for developing more sophisticated analysis and evaluation.

About the exam

Scheme of assessment

The unit test is 1 hour 30 minutes long, and each unit accounts for 50% of the A2 mark (25% of the overall A-level mark).

Exam format

Exam type	Written
Duration	1 hour 30 minutes
Question choice	Section A: 3 questions from a choice of 5 Section B: 1 question from a choice of 3
Question format	Section A: each short-answer question is worth 15 marks Section B: each essay question is worth 45 marks
Question focus	Section A: each question relates to concepts linked to a specific ideology Section B: each question relates to a key issue linked to a specific ideology
Total marks available	90
Overall weighting	50% of total A2 mark (25% of total A-level mark)

Timing

Since the two sections carry the same number of marks, it is recommended that you spend 45 minutes on Section A (15 minutes for each question) and 45 minutes on Section B.

How to answer the questions

Short-answer questions

You will have to answer three from a list of five questions. This means that there will be a question on each of the four ideologies covered in this unit. One of them will have two questions. There is no guarantee or strict rotation as to which ideology will be examined by two questions.

The questions aim to test your understanding of the basic concepts of each ideology. The command words will be 'why', 'explain' or 'what'. They may also test your ability to compare and contrast the views of two different ideologies on a specific concept.

In order to write a good response, you should make sure you do the following:
- Provide a clear definition of the concept.
- Identify two or three main points and then develop them. You may refer to specific individuals who have written about the topic, but do not namedrop just for the sake of it. Use examples to support your argument.
- Make sure you mention any different opinions on concepts and issues relevant to the question between the various sub-traditions of the ideology (liberal nationalism, radical feminism etc.).
- If there are two command words (such as 'how' and 'why'), make sure that you give them equal treatment.
- Remember that there are more marks allocated for analysis and evaluation (7) than for knowledge (5), and balance your answer accordingly.
- Plan the answer with care. Since you will have only about 15 minutes to write each of the answers to this type of question, you must not get carried away in lengthy but unnecessary detail. You can write a fully comprehensive answer within 250 words.

Do not answer questions in reverse order by attempting the essay question before the short answers. The short-answer questions prepare you for the essay question. Candidates who attempt to reverse the order usually end up disadvantaging themselves, and the final short-answer question may end up as a hurried afterthought.

Essay questions

You are required to answer one essay question from a list of three. This means that one ideology will not be covered by an essay question. It is likely — but not guaranteed — that the ideology that 'misses' an essay question will be the one which has two short-answer questions.

- Read the question carefully and make sure you answer that question and only that question.
- Take an essay-style approach, which requires an introduction, an argument and a conclusion.
- The main skill tested is AO2 — evaluation.
- There is no 'right' or 'wrong' answer. You will gain marks for the quality of your argument and conclusion.
- You will be required to evaluate arguments, presenting different points of view to allow synopticity to be addressed. Remember that 12 of the 24 AO2 marks are for synopticity.
- Your introduction should provide a clear definition of key terms used in the question, make clear that you understand the 'point' of the question and outline the argument you intend to develop in the main body of your essay.
- In the argument section of your essay you should make points in a clear sequence, supporting each with appropriate evidence and qualifying where necessary by use of words such as 'however'.
- Your conclusion should be a new paragraph beginning 'In conclusion...'. Then, clearly and briefly, outline the key points that support your conclusion.

Revision and examination preparation

There is no one single effective method of studying, and of revising and preparing for an examination. What you must do to maximise your success is prepare systematically.

To do this, you need to know:
- the key concepts and content explanation for each of the four ideologies
- the number of questions on the paper
- the different types of question (e.g. short-answer and essay questions)
- how much choice you have (e.g. how many short-answer questions and how many essays you have to answer)
- how much time you have to devote to each question
- the specific demands of each type of question

The later sections of this guide go over each of these points in detail. Your teacher may well have already provided you with the details of the specification. You can also find this on the Edexcel website (**www.edexcel.org.uk**), together with sample examination questions and the new-style mark scheme. This is important, as it provides you with a guide as to what is required to gain the highest marks.

Further pointers for study

- Make sure you have made notes on each of the concepts and on all of the core content. If you have not, you run the risk of being confronted by a question you cannot answer. This may then result in you falling into one of the most common traps in examinations, i.e. writing down everything that you know about a subject in the hope that something will be relevant. The best way to avoid this is to have done all the hard work before you reach the revision stage. Make sure you have covered everything, using the specification as a checklist.

- Keep your notes in a folder and in good order. Without this, all the work that you have done will be next to useless and you will not be able to recall the knowledge gained over the preceding months. If there are gaps in the coverage of the specification, make filling them your priority. Your teacher may well have provided material about them in hard copy or electronic forms.

- One form of learning that is especially useful in revision is to work in small groups or teams with your fellow students. It makes it much easier to fill in gaps — even if you have missed a session, others may be able to fill you in on the details. Discussion with others generally leads to greater understanding, as it drives you to clarify your ideas. Another advantage is that some people may have come across new sources (magazine articles, books, or internet references) that are relevant to a particular issue. Most importantly, the process of discussion means that you are no longer facing a problem alone; this enables you to hear other people's ideas, which may in turn produce new ideas of your own. If your school or college runs Moodle, there may well be an online discussion group facility, where you can raise problems with other students or your teacher.

- Be careful how you use the internet. It is an incredibly valuable additional tool for academic study and can be of great value. However, you must not use it as a sole tool. This is especially true for the study of politics, as the internet has become the natural habitat of the polemicist, the obsessive and the conspiracy theorist. Some of the information on the internet is wrong, and it is not always easy to know what is accurate and what is not.

- On the other hand, there is much valuable material on the internet that it would take a long time to find otherwise. You need to develop and use your analytical abilities to avoid the pitfalls. Look for references that you are able to check. Look for internal coherence in arguments. If statements are based on comments such as 'must be', 'it is obvious that', or 'in all probability', it usually means that there is no evidence.

- When revising, be systematic and follow a clear plan. Haphazard, last-minute reading through all your notes is not a good idea.

- Practice answering both short-answer and essay questions under examination conditions. Even if you choose not to tackle some questions in this way, it is still a valuable exercise to write detailed essay plans.

- **Do not** question spot. There is no guarantee of any particular rotation of questions. Many students have been badly caught out by thinking that they can second-guess the examiner.
- Make sure you answer the question that is set, **not** one that you may have revised. Going down that path is another of the most common reasons why many students underperform in examinations. The point of thorough revision is that you prepare yourself to deal with any question that is set.

Remember, examinations are not a trap — they are there to assess how well you can cope with the demands of the specification. If you feel confident that you understand everything in the specification, then you have prepared yourself well and can expect to be awarded a correspondingly high grade.

Content
Guidance

This section of the guide explains what you need to know about the four ideologies studied in this unit: liberalism, conservatism, socialism and anarchism. For each ideology you need to know how the core ideas, doctrines and theories affect views on human nature, the state, society and the economy.

(1) Liberalism

This topic covers the origins and basic premises of liberalism, and discusses the influence of the Enlightenment. It examines the main features, such as individualism and freedom. It also compares classical liberalism with modern liberalism, as well as considering the association of liberalism with democracy, constitutionalism and limited government.

(2) Conservatism

This topic examines the origins of conservatism as a reaction to the Enlightenment. It considers the importance of tradition (and therefore property) to the ideology, and the conservative belief that humans are imperfect. There is explanation of the key concept of an organic society and a comparison of one-nation conservatism, neo-liberalism and neo-conservatism.

(3) Socialism

This topic looks at the emergence of socialism and its development, and how it led to the idea of collectivism and equality of outcome. It examines revolutionary and evolutionary socialism, and the emergence of social democracy. There is coverage of communism and Marxism, and a look at the 'middle way' of neo-revisionist social democracy.

(4) Anarchism

This topic discusses the connections between anarchism and both liberalism and socialism. It focuses on the key ideas of anti-statism and a stateless, utopian society. There is discussion of the rejection of conventional political practice, as well as comparison between individualist and collectivist anarchism.

Liberalism

Origins

Liberalism's origins lie in the European intellectual movement known as 'the Enlightenment'. The time frame of this movement is vague, but the core period during which most of the principal works were produced was between 1720 and 1800. However, there were also some 'proto-Enlightenment' figures, such as Sir Isaac Newton, who did flourish before this time and combined Enlightenment features with those of the earlier period.

Stripped to its core, the Enlightenment altered European thought in two fundamental ways:
- It changed beliefs in the nature of **causation** — what makes things happen. Acts of God were replaced by the laws of science (for the physical world) and the laws of nature (for human society).
- It changed beliefs in the **source of knowledge** from divine revelation (as in the Bible) to human rationality.

To slightly oversimplify the change: in 1649 King Charles I was executed because he infringed the laws of God; in 1793 King Louis XVI was executed because he had infringed the rights of man.

All the ideologies studied at A2 either flow out of the Enlightenment or were created in direct opposition to its principles.

The French Revolution of 1789–99 was seen at the time (and since) as the culmination of the Enlightenment process. The American Revolution of 1776–83 was another definitive Enlightenment event. It was directed by a number of men who not only invoked Enlightenment values but who also were significant Enlightenment intellectuals themselves, such as Thomas Jefferson and Benjamin Franklin.

The earliest political group who called themselves liberals were the 'Liberales' — a group of officers who attempted to force King Ferdinand of Spain to implement a constitution in 1819. However, it is clear that the core elements of the ideology were in place before that, and provided the ideological basis for the key figures in the American and French revolutions.

These core elements include all humans possessing the capacity for rational thought. This means that the autonomous human is the centre of existence. This generates a number of concepts that are required to produce a society in which an autonomous and rational human can flourish.

By virtue of this, liberalism is an **idealist** and **universalist** ideology. This means that liberalism holds that its principles are true at all times and in all places. They exist independently and outside the specific reality of any time or society.

Individualism

Individualism is the most fundamental feature of liberalism relating to human nature. It is the unique feature that distinguishes it from the other ideologies discussed in this guide.

For liberals, individualism means that the individual is the key to all human existence. What sets humanity apart from all other living beings is that each individual possesses his or her own self-awareness, personality, capabilities and (most importantly) free will with which to decide his or her own fate.

This is in complete contrast to collectivism, which views individuals as being bound together by common bonds. These bonds are of various kinds — basic humanity, class, religion, nationality or ethnicity — but whatever they may be, the individual is subordinate to them. Originally liberals saw any kind of collectivism as being essentially hostile to individual rights and liberty. However, the later development of modern liberalism (see below) adopted a more sympathetic attitude towards collectivism, seeing human nature as having a dual character — being both individualist and collective.

From this it followed that the ideal society is one constructed around a mass of autonomous, rational individuals. This is often called 'atomic individualism'. This metaphor likens society to a mass of separate and distinct atoms, each of which can exist by itself. Society has to be organised to benefit these autonomous individuals, and their needs must be prioritised over any collective body. This is known as 'ethical individualism'.

'Egotistical individualism' emphasises aspects of self-interest and self-reliance. Individuals are driven by their own needs and a desire to rely on themselves rather than on a group, society or the state. This version is a core feature of contemporary neo-liberalism. 'Developmental individualism' argues that individuals desire to realise their potential to the full. This is an aspect of modern liberalism first put forward by T. H. Green (1836–82).

These ideas have implications for the state. The state constitutes an inherent threat to individual autonomy as it controls human behaviour, taking responsibilities away from individuals and restricting their freedom to act. Liberals have therefore argued that it should be strictly limited in its scope and powers.

However, liberals do believe that a state is necessary. It should be a 'nightwatchman state', protecting individuals from harm. Adam Smith (1723–90) said that it had only three legitimate functions: maintaining a system of justice, defence against foreign aggression, and maintaining public works. John Locke (1632–1704) justified this under social-contract theory. Individuals surrender a small part of their autonomy to a state so that stable social life can continue. The state can only exist because individuals agree to it existing.

Freedom

This aspect of human nature is closely linked to that of the autonomous individual. Autonomy implies that the individual must be free of all restraints. The only acceptable restraints are those which prevent the individual from curtailing the freedom of others. Because individuals have the power of reason, they are able to rule themselves. There is no justification for restricting freedom on the basis of people 'not being fit to govern themselves'.

Mature individuals should be free to decide their own fate. There should be no legal or social restraint on their choice of occupation, residence, religious faith and ability to practice this. There should be no confines on their ability to express themselves (freedom of speech) or to associate with others (to form political parties or any other association). They are free to own property. This is the foundation of the liberal view of the economy. This kind of freedom was described as **negative freedom** by the philosopher Isaiah Berlin (1909–97). The state has no right to infringe these freedoms.

Freedom was one of the main ideological foundations of the campaign against slavery from the 1750s. It was argued that to allow *any* individuals to be legally enslaved undermined freedom as a universal principle. Following this line of argument, these specific freedoms became the basis of what are now called **civil rights** and **human rights**. The European Convention on Human Rights and the UN Charter of Human Rights both draw heavily on this concept, and develop it further than the classical liberals.

This view was criticised by Green, and others. They said that it accepted gross social inequalities, and did not allow most people the chance to exercise freedoms. A population degraded by poverty, who could only struggle to survive on a daily basis, was not free at all. True freedom could only exist where people have a positive opportunity to realise their potential and their personality. Since private enterprise did not do this, the state had to step in to make it possible. This meant a system of universal education and other welfare provisions, such as sickness and unemployment insurance. This was later termed **positive freedom** by Berlin.

Both classical and modern liberals support the concept of freedom. However, they differ because of the implications for the state of the different definitions.

Classical liberals' view of negative freedom saw a role for the state that was limited to keeping the peace and providing defence against invasion. Neo-liberal theorists such as Spencer and Hayek argued that positive freedom, by creating social welfare programmes requiring high taxation, infringed the freedom to hold and use your own property on a scale that compromised the essential nature of freedom. They advocated a minimal state that enables the free market to function to its freest extent. The state should make sure that imperfections in the market are not allowed to develop.

Positive freedom implies a much more interventionist state, which has to provide a universal system of education and welfare support to prevent people being consumed by poverty. In their view, taxation for these purposes is necessary, fair and beneficial. The state has a duty to regulate economic and social activity to ensure that positive freedom can be achieved.

Classical liberalism

This was the original form of liberalism and is founded on the concepts of individualism in its 'atomic' or 'egotistical' variants. Classical liberals believe that humans have inalienable natural rights, which they possess *because* they are human (or because God has given them, in the view of religious believers). These are universal rights, which no state or social group has the right to take away. They provide the basis for the UN Declaration on Human Rights and the European Convention on Human Rights.

An important early version of classical liberalism was utilitarianism, developed by the philosopher Jeremy Bentham (1748–1832). It is often summed up in the phrase 'the greatest happiness for the greatest number'. Utilitarians believe that imperfections in society can be removed by legal and administrative action. Since this implies state regulation of a limited kind, it has often created tensions with other liberals. Utilitarian measures sometimes required increased taxation, as in the proposals for sewage systems to improve public health. This ran up against liberal objections to high taxation levels and state regulation of private behaviour.

Classical liberals believe in negative freedom with a minimal, or nightwatchman, state. There must be the fewest possible restrictions on individual behaviour consistent with the maintenance of a stable society. Since property ownership is a core freedom, liberals believe that the state has an absolute duty to protect property. This means the establishment of a system of law to regulate property ownership and transfer, a system of justice to punish those who infringe property rights, and a system of government that will protect property rights.

Classical liberals believe in the free market as the correct method for organising economic activity. This is linked with the laissez-faire philosophy that governments should regulate economic activity as little as possible. This principle was developed by Adam Smith, the founder of modern economics, in his book *The Wealth of Nations* (1776). This theory is that the market will regulate itself through the operation of the laws of supply and demand to produce the best possible outcomes.

Their individualist beliefs lead them to reject large-scale welfare. From the beginning they have argued that welfare destroys wealth that has been created by the enterprising and encourages immoral and dissolute behaviour by individuals who are led into dependency on the state. It is also immoral to deprive the enterprising of the just rewards for their hard work by taxation to support those who do not work to maintain themselves and their families.

Modern liberalism

One of the central points made by people who became the founders of modern liberalism was that formal equality did not create actual equality. It did not provide true equality of opportunity because it permitted vast inequalities of wealth and living standards, denying many individuals the opportunity to develop their abilities and gain the true reward for their merit. Some individuals were unjustly exercising their power to deny many others the chance to fulfil their potential.

'Self-fulfilment' became the modern liberals' justification for promoting a new kind of equality: **developmental equality**. This demanded that society should act to ensure that all individuals have a real chance to achieve success in life, and to realise their abilities. This became the justification for an **interventionist state**, which included expanded state education and other welfare provisions to raise up disadvantaged individuals. Later it developed into a theory of a **managed economy**, where the state has a duty to ensure that the health of the economy is not left vulnerable to dysfunctions of the free market.

Modern liberalism argues that humans have a dual nature — both individual and collective. This idea was first put forward by T. H. Green, and later developed by D. G. Ritchie and others. They advocated a form of individualism (developmental) that could only be realised in contemporary conditions by the means of an interventionist state. Poverty and social deprivation made it impossible for many individuals to achieve the position in society that their intrinsic merits deserved. These merits had to be developed by some form of collective action.

It drew upon the ideas of possibly the most influential liberal thinker of all time, John Stuart Mill (1806–73). Mill distinguished two kinds of pleasure, higher and lower. Unlike many classical liberals, Mill believed that everyone has the ability to develop their sensibilities so that they can appreciate 'high culture': music, art and literature.

From this developed the concept of positive freedom (see earlier section on freedom), which produced a revision in the liberal view of the state. A state providing for the self-realisation of individuals through universal education and welfare measures to insure against sickness and unemployment is a benevolent state. It supports individuals, rather than oppressing them. By producing a level playing field, free from wealth and class advantage, the state can create real equality of opportunity.

The twentieth-century UK welfare state drew directly on these ideas. The Liberal government of 1905–15 introduced old-age pensions, national insurance and a number of other measures. Lord Beveridge, who wrote the famous 1942 report that formed the basis of the postwar welfare state, was a liberal who had worked on the 1905–15 reforms.

Modern liberalism developed further with the theories of **economic management** of J. M. Keynes (1883–1946). He argued that the Great Depression of the 1930s showed that the free market was not self-regulating but dysfunctional. He proposed state management of economic activity by a combination of government spending and fiscal policies to regulate the level of economic demand. This was the dominant economic theory from 1945 until the economic crisis of the mid 1970s. Economic management experienced a revival with the onset of the global economic crisis of 2007–08.

The success of neo-liberalism, based on classical liberal principles, has produced tensions within modern liberalism. With the success of free-market globalisation, many liberals qualified their endorsement of state action. Following the lead of the Clinton administration (1993–2001), many have adopted the 'hand up, not a hand out' principle to welfare. This restricts the positive freedom aspect to finding employment, which is closer to utilitarianism than core modern liberalism.

Liberalism and democracy

Democracy is the ultimate political form of ideological liberalism. It refers to the ideal form of state, and is common to both classical and modern liberals.

Liberals see democracy as the ultimate protection against tyranny. Free and fair elections, with open competition between political parties, allow governments to be removed if they have lost the confidence of the electorate. There must be no artificial restrictions placed on the formation of parties, or on their ability to contest elections. They must also be fair, in the sense that no one (usually the incumbent executive) should interfere in the electoral process.

Democracy also implies that each individual is equal as an elector: one person, one vote. This gives everyone an equal influence on how the country is governed and how the legislature is composed. Since voting is done by individuals, it constrains the collective pressures of groups within society. This is why liberals are opposed to any notion of vote 'banks' or 'blocks', or practices such as 'collective voting' where people vote on the basis of decisions taken by leaders of families or communities. Such practices are seen as undermining individual autonomy and being essentially undemocratic.

Democracy is also a means of personal development. Deciding how to cast your vote should be a process of rational thought. Having read the various manifestos, listened to and possibly questioned candidates, the electors then consider the arguments and make their decision as to where they will cast their vote. The electoral process educates electors about important issues and improves their ability to participate in the future.

Liberalism was not always necessarily associated with democracy. In the mid-nineteenth century, Robert Lowe and others saw democracy as a potential threat. Linking rationality with education, they wished to restrict democratic rights to those qualified to use them. They maintanted that the uneducated masses were not capable of properly exercising the right to vote. Echoes of this attitude persisted until 1965 in the southern states of the USA, many of which employed literacy tests to exclude black citizens from electoral registers.

The most common liberal argument against democracy is that it will produce the 'tyranny of the majority'. A temporary majority in an assembly (which may not even be a majority of the electorate) could enact measures that restricted the human rights of members of the minority. It is easy to imagine how these could be discriminatory on several bases: religion, class or ethnicity.

Some liberals, such as Lowe, argued that a democracy would be essentially collectivist. He feared that the working class would vote as a block in favour of candidates committed to socialist policies of nationalisation and state control. The result of this would be an expansion of government and state regulation of all aspects of life. The high levels of taxation necessary to sustain this would undermine economic prosperity, and the dead hand of government bureaucracy would suffocate individual enterprise and innovation.

Constitutionalism and limited government

Constitutionalism is a central feature of both the classical and modern liberal theory of the state. Although liberals celebrate the individual and the individual's qualities, there is also an element of fear. Since individuals act in their own enlightened self-interest, there is always the potential danger that individuals (or groups of individuals) might use political power to pursue their own interests to the extent that they act against the interests of all other individuals. In the worst cases they will become oppressive. This was the liberal explanation and criticism of Napoleon. The fear of individual self-interest in government is often summed up by the famous maxim of the philosopher Lord Acton: 'Power tends to corrupt, and absolute power corrupts absolutely.'

To discourage corruption, liberals insist that every state should have a constitution — a set of laws and regulations covering how the state should be governed. Following the ideas of the French philosopher Montesquieu, the framers of the US Constitution created a series of internal checks and balances. The constitution sets down clearly defined powers and responsibilities of each part of the state, and the procedures by which these powers and responsibilities should be exercised. The three powers of the state — executive, legislature and judiciary — are rigorously separated. If any branch attempts to exceed its authority, prescribed procedures exist for the others to take action against this.

In the legislature, there are two 'houses', separately elected, each with specific powers. These serve to check a temporary majority in one enacting illiberal measures. In addition, each state of the USA has clearly delineated powers and responsibilities that cannot be removed by the federal government. Power is thus diffused through a number of institutions, making tyrannical government less likely.

These powers and responsibilities are 'entrenched', that is, they cannot be removed by a temporary political majority in the executive or legislature. Since amendments may be required from time to time, procedures were put in place for these to be made. These require the repeated assent of the institutions of state.

In this way, the US Constitution provides a model for a state to protect itself against the possibility that power might be seized by a corrupt or dictatorial individual. Liberal opinion often criticises the UK for its 'uncodified' constitution. For liberals, the major defect is that nothing is entrenched. Any passing parliamentary majority can (in theory) enact any legislation it likes. The UK constitutional principle is that 'no Parliament can bind its successors'.

Many other constitutions have been written following the US model. In 1949 the constitution of the new Federal Republic of Germany (FRG) was drafted precisely to enshrine these liberal features. With the intention of preventing a repetition of the Nazis' legal seizure of power, all powers of each part of the state are entrenched. There are no emergency provisions for suspension of any part of the constitution, unlike the infamous Article 48 of the Weimar Republic's constitution that was the Nazi's legal device for obliterating parliamentary democracy and all civil rights. The FRG's constitution is arguably the ultimate expression of liberal democracy and constitutionalism.

Conservatism

Origins

As much as liberalism is the product of the Enlightenment, modern conservatism came out of the hostile reaction to that movement. The event that was the catalyst to the creation of modern conservatism was the political culmination of the Enlightenment: the French Revolution.

The intellectual origin of British conservative thought for the last 200 years was Edmund Burke's (1729–97) *Reflections on the Revolution in France*, written in 1790. Ironically, Burke up to that time had been a typical Enlightenment rationalist and the leading intellectual of the party of parliamentary authority against the Crown — the Whigs. He had made his career by relentlessly pursuing aspects of overbearing state authority. His arguments, therefore, were not serving a vested interest, but were the product of a fundamental ideological process.

Conservative thought in the most general sense had been emerging in Europe for a hundred years. Ruling-class figures attempted to give an ideological aspect to the resistance of autocratic monarchies to demands for responsible (and sometimes representative) government. In Britain this took the form of 'Church and King' Toryism. This was a crude ideology based on the received (or prescribed) authority of the Church of England and the monarchy, and stemmed from the issues on which the Civil War of 1642–49 was fought. In the 1730s it was given a more sophisticated twist by Henry St John, Viscount Bolingbroke, who developed the theory of the 'patriot king'.

Bolingbroke proposed a monarch who would represent the entire people and protect them from the oppression of a corrupt oligarchy (in his view, the governing Whig Party). In this, he was echoing some of the views of the philosopher Thomas Hobbes (1588–1679), who viewed the monarchy as representing the whole of society in his own person. Hobbes is sometimes seen as a precursor of the authoritarian version of conservatism, although he was a much more ambivalent figure than that.

Bolingbroke's patriot king was an ideological and political dead-end. Toryism in Britain was rescued from irrelevance by Burke and William Pitt the Younger, neither of whom ever described themselves as Tory. They gave conservatism in Britain distinctive features, which will be discussed later.

From them came what is called 'traditional' conservatism, later modified by Benjamin Disraeli (1804–81) into what became known as 'one-nation' conservatism. The final variant emerged in the mid-1970s as the 'New Right'. This is especially controversial, as many conservatives dispute that it is really a form of conservatism at all.

Tradition

This is a view of society based on the inheritance of institutions and practices from the past. It implies that respect is given to these, and that they will be maintained in the present and transmitted to the future. Inheritance was at the core of Edmund Burke's ideas. For him, institutions transmitted from the past were what held society together. They guaranteed the rights and privileges of all sections of society. It is *the* core concept of so-called 'traditional conservatism'.

Without these traditions, society would be like a boat cut adrift from its moorings. There could be no guarantee of anyone's rights, freedoms or property. It was this feature of the first year of the French Revolution that so alarmed Burke. The men who controlled the government were moderate liberals, trying to produce a French version of the British constitutional monarchy. Nevertheless, Burke saw their policy as a disastrous experiment. The British system was the product of *British* history and society. By cutting themselves off from their own past, the French liberals could not simply recreate the British system in France. Instead, they were only preparing the ground for a tyranny far worse than the one they had destroyed.

This became the conservative explanation for Napoleon, after he established first a constitutional dictatorship and then his own monarchy in the Empire. By removing tradition (pre-existing institutions), there was now no barrier to unlimited tyranny. The same argument was used by conservatives in the twentieth century to explain and criticise the dictatorship of Stalin in the Soviet Union. By destroying all the existing social and political institutions, the Russian revolutionaries had paved the way for a totalitarian dictatorship.

Therefore tradition — monarchy, organised religion, family and all other social and political institutions — is the basis of *any* stable society. It is legitimate because it has existed and functioned for many generations. In colloquial terms, it is justified because it works. Any institution that continues to function properly should not be altered because it does not fit with some universal theory or contemporary fad. To use another phrase, 'if it's not broke, don't fix it'.

This is the basis of the contemporary conservative opposition to constitutional reform in the UK. Institutions that have stood this test of time (such as the House of Lords) should not be abolished or radically altered. Attempts to do so, especially random, half-hearted ones, will simply be dysfunctional and threaten the entire constitutional stability of the UK.

On the international field this explains conservative opposition to attempts to spread democracy. Conservatives argue that this will undermine and disrupt the societies that are the subject of these actions. Such attempts will produce disorder and new tyrannies, not liberal freedom. This was the reason why some conservatives opposed the Iraq War of 2003. They later claimed to be justified because the overthrow of Saddam Hussein had produced an ungovernable state, prone to disintegration and producing regional instability and conflict.

Human imperfection

Conservatives usually perceive human imperfection as having three aspects: psycho-logical, moral and intellectual.

Psychological imperfection is rooted in the conservative view of **human nature**. Rejecting liberal rational individualism, conservatives see humans as weak and security-seeking. They are dependent on social frameworks to make sense of society and their role in it. Without social support they are liable to suffer psychological collapse.

A hierarchy deals with this problem. Every individual has his or her place with its own clear role, and rights as well as duties. This anchors all individuals and calms their fears of being cut adrift and made isolated. A hierarchy dominated by what Disraeli described as 'natural leaders' is calculated to produce social peace and harmony. People are ready to defer to their betters because their betters are fitted and trained to perform their role at the top of society. Conservatives believe that humans do not have confidence in people who try to perform tasks that they are not fitted to by their position in the hierarchy — their 'station in life'.

Tradition also helps to deal with a lack of security. People are reassured by familiar institutions that have stood the test of time. Success in the past seems to guarantee success in the future. As the world becomes increasingly perilous and uncertain, insti-tutions such as the monarchy, parliament, the law and the armed forces become points of stability for insecure people.

Moral imperfection flows from the idea that, left to themselves, humans will easily fall into socially disruptive behaviour. At worst, this will be unrestrained criminality. Conservatives think that most humans lack innate moral values. They do not under-stand the need for social order and for respect for the rights of others. There needs to be authority exercised over them to ensure social order. The state has a duty as well as a right to exercise authority. Without this, society will lack direction and all groups will attempt to get an advantage over each other. Left to themselves, they will lead society to the point of disintegration. All social institutions will become dysfunctional.

Conservatives believe that humans are intellectually imperfect because they reject the view that individuals are rational. The world is so complex as to be beyond the understanding of ordinary humans. This is one conservative justification for religion: it gives meaning to an incomprehensible world. We are provided with explanations as to how we arrived here, why events occur and the purpose of our existence. Traditional institutions and practices are an expression of these explanations.

However, the neo-liberal interpretation of conservatism fundamentally disagrees with these views. It is one of the most basic disputes within the conservative tradition.

Organic society

A key concept of both traditional and one-nation conservatism is the organic society. It is a metaphor, comparing society with a human body. A functioning body requires all its limbs and organs to be healthy and operating in harmony. In the same way, any healthy society requires all its constituent parts to be healthy and fulfilling their proper roles in harmony with each other.

This implies conditions of social peace between classes and other groups in society. Social conflict would mean that the parts of the body were acting against each other. Thus shared values are essential, because these will prevent social conflict. This is why many conservatives oppose the diversity and pluralism of modern multicultural society. They argue that it legitimises values and practices that are in conflict with traditional British values of respect for the law, the monarchy and national identity; in doing so, it sows the seeds of future social conflict.

Hierarchy is essential to such a society. In a hierarchy, authority flows down the structure, while obedience and deference flow up. This is often illustrated as a pyramid or a ladder. The classic example is the Roman Catholic Church. There are a large number or organisational layers, and any individual in one layer owes unquestioning obedience to superiors. Equality between the levels of a hierarchy is both impossible and undesirable. The structure could not operate under conditions of equality. Superiors have a right *and* a duty to exercise authority over those beneath them.

Duty and obligation are essential aspects of hierarchy. They keep the society unified and functional. All levels have the duty to fulfil their allotted roles and to obey the rightful instructions of those set in authority over them. Everyone has to do their duty. Those at the top of society have a special obligation to carry out their responsibilities to those lower down the hierarchy. These are a consequence of having power, wealth and status. Sometimes referred to by the French term *noblesse oblige,* this aspect is particularly stressed by one-nation conservatives.

The same approach was taken by Christian Democracy in Western Europe after 1945. Emphasising social solidarity, it justified state regulation of the economy and social-welfare programmes on the need to keep society prosperous and stable.

In contrast, neo-liberal conservatives from the New Right see society as being formed from individuals, capable of independent rational behaviour, at least in the free market. There is a variation based on the economy. The health of society comes from allowing these individuals to compete in the free market. Therefore, there is no fixed and timeless combination of 'limbs and organs' to protect. Instead there is an 'atomic society', where the metaphor is one of millions of free-flowing individuals like so many free-moving and independent atoms.

Property

Burke used property as a metaphor to justify tradition. We should respect traditional institutions because we inherit them just as we inherit property. In making this point, Burke underlined property as an essential conservative foundation of society. It is a key feature for all types of conservatives.

Until 1867, property was the qualification for possessing political rights in the UK: the right to vote and the right to stand for elective office. The justification was that it constituted the real value of society. Without property, an individual had no stake in society and existed purely for the convenience of the property owners. Someone without property was of no substance.

Property became a traditional institution. It had proved its worth by being the means for society to undertake production and exchange. It allowed the productive power of society to expand. The joint-stock company, an expression of property rights, was the most effective means of organising productive power yet created. Property was the core of social hierarchy. It enabled the top levels to maintain their position. It enabled the exercise of authority through these institutions and ultimately in the armed force that it nourished.

Property also has ramifications for humans. Naturally wayward and irrational, the possession of property has a transformational effect on people. With the interest in society that property confers, humans are less likely to resort to crime, perceiving that respecting the property rights of others safeguards their own property. People will become supportive of the structure of society, which has enabled them to become property owners. Members of society will become respectful of prescribed authority, because it protects their own property. They will experience pressure to act prudently, because of the need to conserve their property. People will become supportive of the family, because it is the means to transmit their property to their heirs.

Thus property has an almost mystical quality for conservatives, as it mitigates the worst features of human nature. It provides security in an insecure world. This is why after 1945 conservatives in the UK promoted the idea of a 'property-owning democracy'. By giving large numbers of lower-middle-class and working-class people property (usually their own homes), they gain a stake in society. This brings social stability by turning them into supporters of the existing social order (the traditional and one-nation argument). It would also provide an incentive to increase the overall prosperity of society: the neo-liberal argument.

As a free-market ideology, neo-liberalism sees property ownership by individuals as a prime objective. It is a reward to innovative and risk-taking individuals for their hard work. Each such individual has a right to enjoy the rewards of his or her labours, free from onerous restrictions and taxation.

One-nation conservatism

One-nation conservatism stems from old Tory origins of tradition, organic society and, most of all, paternalism. The corresponding metaphor comes from innate, sometimes God-given, roles in the family. The father is to be head of the household. While this gives him authority over the rest of the family, it also imposes on him a number of duties. He has to 'provide' for the family — a place to live, food, clothing, and the other necessities of life. He has to give proper guidance to other family members, especially his children. This can include whom to marry, or a choice of career. To fail to perform any of these duties will threaten the proper functioning of the entire family unit.

It fits well with the traditional conservative view of human nature, especially the security-seeking aspect and the concept of organic society. It also sits well with the conservative view of hierarchy. Those at the head of society have an essential duty to care for the inferior ranks. This is often expressed by the French term *noblesse oblige* — the obligations of rank. Individual aristocrats often, but far from always, felt a duty to care for their tenants and employees in modest material ways. This idea was the intellectual justification for charitable and philanthropic works.

Disraeli took this idea and used it as the central justification for limited social reform by conservatives. He staked out his view of British society in his early novels *Sybil* (1845) and *Coningsby* (1844). Society was divided into two nations: those of prosperity and poverty. This was dysfunctional, and would lead to social disorder. By the time he reached the top of the Conservative Party in the 1860s, Disraeli would contrast the obligations recognised by the natural leaders of society with the insensitive individualism of liberal industrialists, generating the social evils of mid-Victorian Britain.

Social reform to create 'one nation' became a core feature of British conservatism. Social reform appeared spasmodically in Disraeli's government of 1874–80, and was dominant in the period 1945–75. One-nation conservatism developed into the 'middle way' approach of the 1930s — a pragmatic rejection of the free market because of the crisis of the Depression. The state had an obligation to intervene in the economy and to provide welfare services to prevent abject poverty.

In Western Europe, social reform was a central component for Christian Democrats. They drew more on biblical injunctions to care for the sick and needy. The result was the same as in the UK: support for a paternalist state with a fundamental duty to provide for all sections of society through social-welfare schemes. This has proved to be more resilient than its UK counterpart.

Because of their reliance on meritocratic individualism and the transformational effect of the free market, neo-liberals reject all forms of paternalism. They see it as the cause of social and economic stagnation and decay. In both the UK and the USA, neo-liberals made rooting out paternalism a prime objective.

Neo-liberalism

'Neo' is a prefix meaning 'new'. Neo-liberalism, therefore, is a contemporary ideology in the form of certain aspects of classical liberalism. It is based on a view of the economy.

The form that neo-liberalism principally resembles is that of a fundamental emphasis on the free market as the ideal form of social organisation and as a means of solving all central political issues. Its origins lie in the criticisms of the theory of economic management made by exiled members of the Austrian school of economists, such as Frederick von Hayek and Ludwig von Mises (1881–1973). These were developed by the Chicago school, whose most prominent member was Milton Friedman (1912–2006).

All of these critics argued that attempts to regulate the economy through demand management were bound to lead to disaster. The state is not an effective instrument of innovation and wealth creation. Increasing shares of national product taken by the state simply drain resources from the productive private sector of the economy and lead to a situation of stagnation.

Although these ideas were around from the 1940s, during the 'long boom' of 1950–73 they were argued by a minority, prophesying doom from the margins. Their moment came with the global economic crises of 1973–76 and 1979–81. The combination of economic stagnation and massive inflation (30% in the UK in 1975) was beyond the capacity of Keynesian demand management to rectify. Friedman and the Chicago school of economists — he taught at the University of Chicago — had an answer. Governments should use supply-side economics to control inflation through a reduction in the supply of money to the economy. This became known as 'monetarism'.

Their long-term solution was to 'roll back the state'. The state should cease to attempt to manage demand to regulate output and employment. Its proper role was to take measures to increase the supply of resources to the productive private sector of the economy, hence the term *supply-side* economics. The government should do this by reducing the proportion of gross domestic product (the value of all commodities produced in a country in a year) taken by taxation.

This could be achieved by reducing the total amount of state expenditure. The government should release productive assets from state ownership and give control back to the private sector. This led to the privatisation of nationalised industries in Britain in the 1980s and 1990s. This strategy was promoted by international organisations such as the International Monetary Fund and the World Bank after the mid 1990s.

Neo-liberalism also means that regulation of economic activities should be reduced, in order to enable wealth creation to be maximised This means less regulation of areas such as employment law, financial services and credit, and a wide range of trading activities. The idea is that the innovative capabilities of entrepreneurs, risk takers who are the real wealth creators of society, are hampered by over-mighty bureaucratic restraints.

There is a moral aspect to this. In 1944 von Hayek had argued that social welfare and state economic regulation would produce a 'new serfdom'. In this, he followed the 1884 argument of the British liberal philosopher Herbert Spencer. Free individuals would become enslaved and dependent upon the state, compromising their self-reliance and self-respect. By the early 1990s, this had developed into a society seen as being plagued by a 'dependency culture'. Generations of people were becoming reliant on state benefits. The family was being undermined as children were being provided for not by their parents, but by state welfare. Ideas of responsibility and duty, and the desire to create wealth, were being rapidly dissipated. Self-reliance and self-worth were disappearing in ever greater sections of society, which were in turn becoming a permanent burden on the wealth-creators.

The solution was twofold. People who were caught in the demeaning 'dependency culture' had to be weaned off it by restricting their rights to universal and unlimited benefits. Welfare was to be linked to actively seeking employment — what is termed 'welfare to work'.

The other aspect was to promote the alternative 'enterprise culture'. The ideal role models were wealth-creating entrepreneurs such as Sir Alan Sugar and Sir Richard Branson. Individual innovation and risk-taking on a massive scale would re-energise society.

Neo-liberalism was primarily associated with the Conservative governments in the UK in 1979–97 and the Republican administrations in the USA of 1981–93 and 2001–09. However, the emphasis on entrepreneurship and welfare to work (which was promoted by the Clinton administration of 1993–2001) shows that neo-liberalism is not confined to specific political parties. It has been the dominant global ideological feature after the collapse of the USSR in 1991. Globalisation is only the application of neo-liberal principles on an international scale.

Neo-conservatism

This is the second component of the New Right. It can be convincingly argued that it is a mild contemporary form of authoritarianism.

Neo-conservatives saw the crises of the 1970s as primarily a failure of social morality. Order and discipline were being lost because there had been a collapse in respect for authority and the loss of a sense of duty. In Britain, this was blamed on the permissive society of the 1960s. Liberal legislation on social issues encouraged sexual licence and the undermining of the family. The 1965 abolition of the death penalty sent a message that the most serious crime would not attract the ultimate penalty, and so encouraged violence.

The consequence was the social disruption of the late 1960s and 1970s: student protests, militant strikes and racial unrest. The remedy was rigorously to enforce public order. The Thatcher government of the 1980s made a special point of using every legal power to support police action against militant strikes, culminating in the miners' strike of 1984–85. The response by the authorities to the IRA campaign in Northern Ireland was to treat the ring leaders as ordinary criminals. Such controversial action had been justified by Margaret Thatcher in her Cheltenham speech of 1982, where she spoke of the threat from 'the enemy within'.

Neo-conservatism in both the UK and the USA promoted the use of increased punishments, and a consequent increase in the amount of people being incarcerated in prisons. Authority had to be imposed, especially on those sections of society that displayed no respect for the law. After 2001, neo-conservatism used the 'war on terror' to promote and justify increasing security legislation and the need to curtail individual rights through surveillance and special legislation. Proponents argued that society was under such a severe and enduring threat that it was the state's duty to curtail individual rights in the interests of society.

It is important to note that the neo-conservatism associated with the foreign policy of the Bush administration in the USA of 2001–09 has nothing to do with the above definition. The 'neo-cons' were defined by their wish to reconstruct large areas of the world in the image of free-market liberal democracy. They should have been termed 'neo-liberal internationalists', since their objectives were definitely not conservative, as they rejected the idea that societies should be governed according to tradition and inheritance. Their ideas were most similar to the foreign policy followed by Lord Palmerston in the UK in the nineteenth century. Under his leadership, Britain attempted to spread constitutional government internationally through a combination of economic, diplomatic and military power.

Socialism

Origins

The first elements of socialism emerged in the period of conservative reaction following the defeat of Napoleon in 1815. Although liberalism was still the dominant radical ideology, elements which had sought some form of social justice had emerged during the French Revolution. The most notable of these was the 'Conspiracy of the Equals' led by Gracchus Babeuf in 1794.

By the 1830s, groups arguing for separate working-class organisation existed in France (that of Louis-August Blanqui, 1805–81) and in Britain (the Chartists). By the 1840s, such groups were widespread, if not numerous, across Western Europe. The best-known example was the international League of the Just, which in 1847 renamed itself the Communist League at the instigation of two members of its executive committee, Karl Marx (1818–73) and Frederick Engels (1820–95).

By this time, clear features were developing within socialist thought. They rested on attitudes towards capitalism and the ways in which society might be transformed.

Initially, all socialists believed that not only is society unequal but that all wealth is produced by labour. From this, socialists believed that free-market capitalism is a source of inequality and exploitation. The question was what to do about it. There developed essentially two strategies:

(1) Totally destroy capitalism through the abolition of private property. To replace capitalism there should be some form of socialisation of property under democratic control. This view was promoted by Marx and Engels, and by the French tendency influenced by Philippe Proudhon (1809–65).

(2) Reform capitalism to save the interests of all the people. This would involve increased legislation on social conditions, social welfare financed by taxation on the rich, and some limited public ownership of industry. This became the preferred strategy of the British trade unions and significant sections of the socialist movements in Europe (such as the Lassallean movement in Germany).

There was a corresponding debate as to how a socialist outcome should be achieved. Again, there were two main strategies:

(a) Bring about a revolutionary transformation of society. This would involve the destruction of all the existing state institutions and a wholesale reorganisation of all social relations. The existing class system would be abolished. This was 'revolutionary socialism'.

(b) Embrace the institutions of the existing state, and seek to use them to make incremental social reforms. As more states introduced widespread male franchise, this was used as a justification for this approach. Taking Darwinism as a metaphor, this became known as 'evolutionary socialism', also the title of a book by the German Social Democrat Eduard Bernstein (1850–1932).

Most mass socialist parties formed after 1870 were an uneasy compromise between these tendencies. This was shown by the name that many of them chose: 'social democrat'. The exception was the British Labour Party of 1900, where revolutionary support was always marginal.

As a general rule, people who believed in (1) also believed in (a), and those who accepted (2) believed in (b). However, there always was, and still remains, a significant number of socialists who believe that a revolutionary transformation of society can be achieved by using existing political structures. This 'parliamentary road to socialism' was upheld by a minority in the British Labour Party, and by most non-ruling communist parties after 1934.

Communist parties came into existence following the October Revolution in Russia in 1917 and the formation of the Soviet Union. Until then, most socialists had papered over the divisions discussed above, which they were no longer able to do. Every socialist party eventually split, usually with the 'reformist' majority expelling a pro-Soviet minority. These then adopted the old name 'communist', while the now unambiguously evolutionary and reformist parties kept the names 'social democrat' and 'socialist', and in Britain 'labour'.

Social democracy eventually shed all its Marxists elements. As a result, it moved towards a multi-class position, although retaining some orientation towards the working class, if only for electoral reasons. After the success of neo-liberalism in the 1980s, another development occurred. This re-emphasised the appeal to all classes in society, overtly embraced the free market and minimised the elements of social reform and wealth redistribution. This middle path between state-centred social democracy and neo-liberalism is called the 'third way', and was pioneered by New Labour in the UK.

Collectivism

Collectivism follows from socialist views on human nature, the economy and society. Society is organised on a class basis, with a ruling class and an exploited working class. As social beings, humans have to act collectively to cope with this situation. Collectivism came to mean a rejection of the free market, private property and capitalism. It implied state ownership of productive assets and state regulation of the economy.

For socialists, collectivism means that people's consciousness is produced by social conditions, rather than innate human nature. In other words, *nurture* is more important than *nature*. It follows that humans are naturally cooperative. This achieves more in both moral and practical economic terms than competition. In many ways, it provides a way towards an ideal society.

The key mechanism for collective action is the state. In the Marxist view, a state created by the working class will, for the first time, act in the interests of the vast majority of society. Viewed objectively it will act in the interest of everyone, including the former ruling class.

From the mid-nineteenth century, socialists promoted the state as the means to achieve the transformation of society. All variants agreed on this broad point. Revolutionaries wanted to have a new workers' state, having destroyed the existing bourgeois state. Marxists used the Paris Commune of 1871 as their model. Reformists wished to modify the existing state and capture control of it through democratic elections.

Gradually, the reformist promotion of the state led to the emergence of a classless socialism, which was defined by an abstract state-led collectivism, in opposition to liberal individualism. This was the version of socialism that was referred to in the title of the Nazi party. For Hitler, socialism was simply anti-individualism and a rejection of the existing social hierarchy.

Trade Unions

Socialists have attempted to implement collectivism in a number of ways. Trade unions and cooperatives are promoted by all types of socialists. They are most important to evolutionary socialists, since they are able to be integrated into the existing structure of society. State ownership of industry is another aspect, which was widely implemented in Western Europe after 1945. For socialists, industries should be run for the benefit of society as whole, not for profit.

In the Soviet Union after 1929, and in Eastern Europe and China after the Second World War, nationalisation was extended to almost all industries. In the USSR, all agricultural land was collectivised, as it was in China from the mid 1950s to the 1980s. The USSR provided a model for a complete transformation of a backward society into a modern industrial state, using total state control of the economy as a means to achieve this. With the collapse of the USSR in 1991, this collectivist model suffered a widespread ideological defeat. This enabled the USA to push through the creation of the World Trade Organization in 1993, promoting neo-liberal principles (globalisation) at the expense of collectivism.

Equality

Socialists view equality in social, rather than individual, terms. For them, all sections of society should enjoy the same life experiences. This is equality of outcome. Material rewards should be distributed equally across society. This equality is the right of every human being and a matter of justice. People cannot develop their full potential if there are fundamental levels of inequality in society.

There are differences among socialists as to how this should be interpreted and achieved. Fundamentalist socialists insist on absolute equality, that is everybody should have exactly the same amount of material goods and life opportunities. This implies a rigid distribution of goods and services, as well as common ownership of all means of production and other property. Without such common ownership, an absolutely equal distribution would not be possible. The body that usually enjoys this common ownership is the state. It is also the state that supervises the equal distribution of resources and prevents unequal accumulation of wealth returning.

Other socialists only aspire to a *relative* equalising of society. What is most important to them is to remove absolute poverty. If this can be achieved, then a certain level of inequality is acceptable. Therefore, they look to a certain amount of redistribution of wealth through taxation and government spending. The state does not own or control all resources, but adjusts the distribution to iron out large differences in wealth. This approach has been the one of evolutionary or reformist socialists.

Socialists argue that equality does more than meet the demands of justice — it also underpins social stability. Societies with great inequalities of wealth also contain great poverty. These societies are inherently unstable. Eventually the dispossessed sections of society will be able to bear their situation no longer and unrest and revolutions will break out. They point to societies such as Russia, China and Mexico at the beginning of the twentieth century as examples.

Such inequality then led to many years of bitter civil war, with millions dead and widespread destruction in each case. Socialists point to the lack of such instability in societies such as Sweden, which has high levels of social equality. Sweden had decades of Social Democratic Party government after 1932. It combined high taxation levels with redistribution of wealth through a social-welfare system. Supporters of the Swedish model of government argue that this prevented the serious social unrest that was common in the rest of Europe in the twentieth century, while retaining a system of parliamentary democracy, unlike the USSR and the satellite states of Eastern Europe.

Revolutionary and evolutionary socialism

Revolutionary socialism starts from the idea that existing society is based on a ruling class that exploits and oppresses the classes below it. All the institutions of society exist to support and preserve the ruling class. This is especially true of the state in all its forms, even including parliaments.

Parliaments were established by 'bourgeois revolutions' that overthrew autocratic monarchies, such as in the Netherlands, Great Britain and France. These were made in the interests of the commercial bourgeoisie, even if they were made in the name of 'the people'. Therefore, the parliaments are a front through which the ruling class exercises political control through its administration of media and finance.

In the twentieth century, many revolutionary socialists in countries that had not yet had their bourgeois revolutions (especially in Africa, Asia and South America) saw revolution as a means of modernising their countries. They would sweep away obsolete feudal society and colonial collaborators. This anti-colonial socialism hoped to use revolution to modernise developing societies and in one leap create societies that were as prosperous and technologically advanced as existing industrial countries.

Revolutionary socialism always implies a complete transformation of all aspects of society. It requires the total destruction of the existing institutions of the state and their replacement by new revolutionary ones. Such a profound transformation usually means the use of violence, if only because supporters of the existing social order are unwilling to concede their position without a fight to the end. Thus there were prolonged and bitter civil wars in Russia, China and Mexico before the revolutionary forces were victorious.

Evolutionary socialists see the state as a neutral force that it is possible to capture and use for one's own objectives. Following the metaphor taken from Darwin, they see change as coming through a series of small instalments, rather than in a single cataclysmic transformation. Since democracy is seen as a legitimate form of government, changes made using it will be accepted by the ruling class, so avoiding the possibility of social conflict or civil war.

Indeed, since the working class in all its forms is the largest class in society, evolutionary socialists argue that socialism is inevitable. Once members of the working class have been educated to become aware of their position in society, in normal conditions they will automatically vote for the socialist party that represents their interests.

This view has been subject to a number of criticisms. Apart from the fact that many workers have continued to vote for conservative parties, it is said that changes in the nature of industry have led to a reduction in the size of the industrial working class. In order to gain electoral majorities, evolutionary socialists have to appeal to sections of the middle class, who have different interests to the working class.

More importantly, evolutionary socialists' immersion in the electoral process has led them to be corrupted by the desire for power within the system. The need to administer the existing system comes before the ability to bring about the small incremental changes that they hope will eventually transform society. In the end they become 'captured' by the state that they had hoped to change.

Communism and Marxism

The term 'communism' was first used in the 1830s, denoting the aim of destroying the existing class structure of society and the institution of private property, thus transforming the economy. Communism was also profoundly internationalist. All states were viewed by communists as the creatures of their own ruling class. The workers therefore had no interest in their survival. The motto of the Communist League was 'Workers of all countries unite, you have nothing to lose but your chains'. This reflected the idea that class consciousness would wish to overthrow the existing society that exploited and oppressed the workers.

The principles of communism were developed in the Communist Manifesto of 1848, written by Marx and Engels on the instructions of the Executive Committee of the Communist League. The manifesto sets out the theory that all history has been about class conflict, which is represented in the present period as a conflict between the proletariat and the bourgeoisie. In previous historical eras there had been other conflicts, between slave and slave owner, and between feudal lord and bourgeoisie.

These principles were distilled into a programme the same year, for the Communist League in Germany. It was a clear and systematic attack on property rights and the material benefits of social status. For Marx and Engels, the state and all social institutions were a superstructure built on the foundations of the economic relations of society. The bourgoisie possessed the means to produce wealth, and the proletariat only survived by selling its ability to labour.

Communism implies the abolition of all classes. Marx and Engels argued that classes exist because there is a limited amount of resources. This limitation has to be managed by a ruling class, and in order to do this ruling classes create states. In Marx's model, all existing state institutions had to be destroyed and replaced by a worker's state, on the model of the Paris Commune of 1871. This state would be a temporary phenomenon. It would exist to prevent a counter-revolution by the old ruling class and to create the conditions for a transformation into a classless society. Marx and Engels envisaged that this would come about because the contradictions of capitalism would throw it into ever more severe crises.

During the transformation of society, capitalism would be replaced by production for use by associated producers. This would bring about a situation of abundance. With abundance, the material basis for distinct classes would disappear.

After the October Revolution in Russia in 1917, social democratic parties split over the question of supporting it. The pro-Soviet groups followed the Bolsheviks in renaming themselves communists. They did so to emphasise their revolutionary nature and to distinguish themselves from their evolutionary/reformist erstwhile comrades. They accused them of capitulating to capitalism and counter-revolution.

In the twentieth century, communism came to represent the most intransigent revolutionary position. This explains why the South African Communist Party (SACP) was the only one in the world which expanded its membership in the 1990s. Across the rest of the world, communist parties disintegrated under the impact of the collapse of the USSR. The SACP escaped this fate because of its history of opposition to the Apartheid regime.

This raises the issue of the USSR and other regimes that were recognised as communist. These included regimes in Eastern Europe and Asia that used other terms, often 'people's democracies', and their parties did not call themselves 'communist', such as the Socialist Unity Party in the German Democratic Republic. To the end, they all claimed to be the authentic inheritors of the October Revolution.

This has always been contested by dissident communists, the best known of whom was Leon Trotsky (1879–1940). He and his supporters argued that Joseph Stalin (1879–1953) and his supporters were counter-revolutionaries who seized power around 1929 and destroyed the legacy of 1917. They created a dictatorship of a privileged bureaucracy, and undermined the international revolution in the interest of a Soviet state that had embraced Russian nationalism. Some Trotskyists went on to argue that the USSR and the other communist states had in fact become a form of 'state capitalism'. The state was acting as a single massive capitalist enterprise, competing on a global scale.

Social democracy

As already mentioned, social democracy was the term used for the compromise between revolutionary and evolutionary socialists in the second half of the nineteenth century. It emerged through the absence of any immediate large-scale social and political crises that put revolution on the agenda.

Faced with a long and indefinite non-revolutionary period, all types of socialists could concentrate on immediate issues of social and political reform. Revolutionary socialists do not oppose these on principle, rather arguing that they will not produce fundamental changes in society. Social democracy allowed most socialist parties to adopt a formal Marxist programme, which called for the abolition of capitalism and private property and the establishment of socialism. This was combined with undertakings that were purely evolutionary: electoral work, civil-rights campaigns, cooperation and trade-union activity.

This compromise was shattered by a leading member of the German Social Democratic Party (SPD), Eduard Bernstein. He lived in Britain for 2 years in the 1890s, and collaborated with the Fabian socialists Beatrice (1858–1943) and Sydney Webb (1859–1947). When he returned to Germany, he outraged many SPD members with a series of articles which were later published in book form as *Evolutionary Socialism* (1899).

In these articles Bernstein maintained that Marx had been wrong to argue that capitalism was doomed to collapse. He said that industrialisation showed that it could surmount any crisis. He also disagreed with Marx that capitalism was irredeemably exploitative of the working class. He said that experience demonstrated a steady rise in working-class living standards. Capitalism could be reformed and 'humanised'.

For this he was bitterly attacked by Rosa Luxemburg (1871–1919), the SPD's rising economist. She criticised him for abandoning the key principles of socialism and capitulating to the ruling bourgeoisie. He was also criticised by the SPD's leading theoretician, Karl Kautsky (1854–1938). Kautsky was known as 'the Pope of Marxism' because of his command of Marxist theory — he had been the literary executor of Engels. His criticisms, however, were of a technical nature. He happily coexisted in the SPD with Bernstein for the next 30 years.

The compromise was finally shattered by the October Revolution. As a result, since the 1920s social democracy has been completely associated with evolutionary socialism. Although many parties took their time to shed their formal Marxist stance (the SPD only did so in 1959), from that period all social democrats embraced reform rather than revolution, and saw the path to socialism lying through the institutions of parliamentary democracy. All dropped the abolition of private property as an aim. Since 1991 many evolutionary elements have disappeared as well, as many (but far from all) social democrats move to a third-way position embracing (with varying enthusiasm) neo-liberal globalisation.

British social democracy was unusual in never having a significant Marxist element. Its mass base came from the reformist trade unions, and its intellectual frame came from the Fabian Society. The Fabians were committed to gradual social reform and increased social efficiency through the action of the state, directed by experts like themselves. This has remained the dominant aspect of British social democracy, expressed through the Labour Party.

One key aim of British social democracy has been equality of outcome. This means that people should have the same life experience, no matter what their social origin.

It was to be achieved through a universal system of state welfare and redistribution of wealth through taxation. This strategy was articulated by Anthony Crosland (1918–76) in his book *The Future of Socialism* (1956), and in recent years has been defended by Roy Hattersley, former Deputy Leader of the Labour Party.

Hattersley has engaged in open debate with Gordon Brown and other New Labour figures over this. Brown criticised Hattersley for holding to an outdated idea, and counterposed a socialist form of equality of opportunity. This was based on his programmes for increasing the skills base of the working population in order to improve their earning capacity.

Since 1994 the 'third way' has been the dominant force in the Labour Party in the form of the New Labour project of Gordon Brown, Tony Blair and Peter Mandelson. The change was signified by the amendment of Clause 4 of the party's constitution. The original 1918 'old Labour' version had referred to widespread nationalisation. This was entirely dropped from the 1994 revision, which replaced it with general statements about achieving more together than alone.

Neo-revisionist social democracy

The neo-revisionist version of social democracy has been posed as a 'middle way' between the absolute free-market strategy of the New Right and the state-centred world view of social democracy. It was first successfully pioneered in the UK by the Labour Party after 1994, and is also referred to as the 'third way'. It has been adapted in various guises by social democratic parties across the world. It addresses the issues of society, the state and the economy.

The driving force for the development of the third way was the apparent decisive global success of neo-liberalism by the early 1990s. On an international scale this was marked by the collapse of the Soviet Union in 1991. The Soviet state-centred model of social and economic development vanished with it. In the UK, this was accompanied by an unexpected fourth consecutive election victory for the Conservative Party in 1992. To many social democrats it appeared that the traditional principles of social democracy would never regain popular support, since they did not meet the realities of the modern globalised economy.

Although Gordon Brown had been outlining aspects of what became the third way since 1988, the New Labour project only began to emerge clearly after 1992. Its strategic direction was to embrace the changes in the global economy created by the success of neo-liberalism in the 1980s. This meant accepting the role of the free market as the decisive force for wealth creation and abandoning the redistribution of wealth through taxation. Social equality became linked to the ability to work in jobs that were highly skilled and therefore better paid. This would produce improved living standards and a more equal society.

In pursuing this, Brown was following the policies of Robert Reich, Secretary of Labor in the first Clinton administration (1993–97). It explains the New Labour slogan

'Education, education, education' and the 'New Deal' welfare strategy aimed at getting young people into work.

It also meant the use of the private sector in the provision of public services. This comes in two forms:
- **Public finance initiative** (PFI) schemes, where the private sector builds and owns new state assets (especially schools and NHS hospitals), and often manages them.
- **Public–private partnerships** (PPP), where private firms manage existing public assets on behalf of the state (such as the London Underground).

Pioneered in the UK, these are now being employed on a widening international scale by governments, many of whom describe themselves as socialist, such as those of India and South Africa. In South Africa, this strategy is being led by NEPAD (New Economic Plan for African Development). Initiated by an agreement between the UK and South African governments, it has pioneered a strategy for economic development which involves embracing neo-liberal principles, including the large-scale privatisation of public assets.

Embracing globalisation also meant reducing the link with the working class. The third way, especially in the New Labour form, means an attempt to create a 'big tent', in which sympathetic people from any social class can enter. This has required abandoning equality of *outcome* in favour of equality of *opportunity*, an essentially liberal principle. The third way stresses 'social inclusivity' — the bringing of all groups in society into the general fold of prosperity and harmony. This has developed into the idea of 'asset-based egalitarianism' — meaning that equality should be derived from the ownership of property. The third way has no dispute with great wealth, as long as the acquisition of this wealth assists the raising of the overall prosperity of society.

The main difference between the third way and the New Right is over its view of society. Rejecting the neo-liberal atomic individualist view, the third way sees society as a collective unit. Lack of social solidarity will undermine society and produce increasing disorder. Individuals have responsibilities and duties to each other and to society as a whole. This has meant support for communitarian initiatives for greater social cooperation (such as parental involvement in schools) and increased public spending on new assets. It is also behind the strategy of welfare summed up in the slogan 'something for something', and 'a hand up not a hand out'. The receipt of welfare is not simply a right; it confers a duty to society to make yourself ready for work and to seek work.

This approach has led many socialists to accuse the third way of being nothing more than a new form of liberalism. However, Gordon Brown would argue that many of the measures promoted by the Treasury in the period 1997–2007 (educational maintainance grants, the minimum wage, family tax credits and Sure Start) are aimed at improving the life experiences of the poorest and most disadvantaged in society. In this view, they amount to a contemporary form of social reform as profound as any before.

Anarchism

Origins

Anarchism has connections with both liberalism and socialism. Like liberalism, anarchism sees society as being based on the sovereign, rational individual. In this sense, it is also a product of the Enlightenment. Most anarchists are hostile to religion, especially organised religion. They see it as a means to enslave humans by superstition and prejudice, in the interests of the ruling elite.

Anarchists part company with liberals over their view that *no* authority should be allowed to restrain individuals. This has given anarchism its unique feature, the one that distinguishes it from all the other ideologies discussed here. It has an absolute opposition to *any* form of state. For anarchists, *any* external authority is oppressive.

Rejecting all state authority threw anarchists into conflict with all states at the end of the nineteenth century. So bitter was the conflict that it resulted in extreme violence from all sides. Anarchists assassinated the Empress of Austria, the King of Italy and President McKinley of the USA. Governments ruthlessly suppressed anarchists and there were many executions. It was this period of violent confrontation that gave anarchism its popular reputation for inherent, random violence against all existing institutions.

Differences with socialism were not always clear. Their similarities were a fundamental hostility to existing society, a desire to overthrow the institution of private property and to create an egalitarian society. Pierre Proudhon, one of the early socialist theorists, appears as one of the originators of anarchism. Revolutionary socialists are often close to anarchists in their political practice, parting company over the issue of the state. Revolutionary socialists see the need for a workers' state as an essential tool to reconstruct society and prevent a capitalist counter-revolution.

For an anarchist, a revolutionary state would be as bad as any other. Far from being a shield to a revolutionary movement, it would hinder and eventually repress it. For anarchists, Napoleon and Stalin were neither the products of specific circumstances nor individual aberrations. They were the inevitable consequence of allowing a popular revolution to be captured by a state. As a result, anarchists are often as hostile to socialists as they are to liberals and conservatives. The issue of the state outweighs all others.

Anarchists, therefore, do not form political parties. The discipline inherent in conventional parties is anathema to them. They tend to group themselves together in 'federations'. This term implies a shared world view and principles. It does not follow that there has to be concerted action. In fact, a key anarchist principle is that in political activity there can be no restraint on individuals. Anyone must be free to carry out any action that they see fit.

This is why anarchists who themselves oppose violence as a political method against the state feel obliged to defend those who do. To attempt to restrain or limit such actions would be to violate the fundamental first principle of anarchism. It would be the first step on the long slippery slope to authoritarianism and dictatorship.

Given this common feature, there is a wide range of variations of anarchism. Some of them are suspicious of each other, as their characteristics are not at all compatible.

Anti-statism

As was stated above, the autonomous, rational individual is at the heart of anarchist ideas, and this overrides any collective identity. For most anarchists, these group identities are diversions, created by ruling elites, whose aim is to confuse people and to lead them away from realising their true nature as rational, sovereign individuals. This is most true of the state, which exists to oppress the individual.

This means that it is impossible for well-meaning people to attempt to 'capture' the state for their own purposes. When discussing the Swiss state, Bakunin observed that no matter how well intentioned individuals might be, they would be corrupted by having to act through a system of authority. He was speaking about a bourgeois parliamentary form of government. The liberal state is simply a camouflage for class oppression. Principles such as constitutionalism and consent are used by the ruling class to control the majority of the population.

Anarchists have the same opinion of revolutionary proletarian states. They insist that these must and will turn into instruments of oppression because they exert authority over free individuals. They point to the example of the USSR as a prime example of this. Not only the bourgeoisie but also anarchists and non-Bolshevik socialists were suppressed by the Soviet state.

To classical anarchists such as Bakunin and Malatesta (1853–1932), the only authority that might be valid is one that is voluntarily accepted by an individual. This, however, is of a very specific and limited nature. This kind of authority would be like that of the experienced craftsperson passing on the skills of the trade to an apprentice. This authority only comes from the craftperson's own inherent capabilities, while it is only voluntarily accepted by the apprentice for the purpose of acquiring knowledge and skills, and can be relinquished at any time. Such authority is ascriptive and it is instrumental for the acquisition of knowledge, limited in time and purpose, and utterly reliant on the rational decision of the individual alone.

This leads to the second anarchist objection to the state: it is unnecessary as well as undesirable. This comes from their view of human nature. Rational humans need no external authority to make decisions for them or to organise their activity. Any mature human is capable of making any decision, and humans can organise any joint activity. Many anarchists believe that humans are naturally cooperative. They will form and administer voluntary associations for any economic and social endeavour.

Stateless society

The anarchist view of a stateless society is often described as **Utopian**. The term is best known from the title of Sir Thomas More's book, *Utopia* (1516). It has gained the popular meaning of something that is naïve, unrealistic and unsustainable. Technically, it means a perfect society. In that sense, it is a charge to which most anarchists will happily plead guilty.

Anarchists believe that an ideal society is possible because of their view of human nature. In contrast to conservatives, they have an extremely positive view. Even more than liberals and socialists, they think that humans are rational beings. Left to themselves, they recognise the need to treat other humans fairly. Their decisions are not made according to emotion or prejudice, but in a logical fashion leading to a clear judgement.

Anarchists see established society as unnatural. Hierarchy, authority and religion are artificial constructions of elites. Their sole reason for existence is to perpetuate the rule of those elites, by oppressing and confusing the mass of the population. The purpose of anarchism is to free people from these false allegiances and superstitious beliefs. Once freed, the true nature of humans will reassert itself. Natural rationality and morality will re-emerge. Anarchists point to altruism, acts undertaken by people with no prospect of any gain for themselves. They say that the widespread extent of altruism, and the approval given to altruistic acts, clearly shows that even under the oppressive and deformed conditions of contemporary society, the true nature of humanity keeps breaking through.

Individualist anarchists argue that humans do not require the security of any collective or social institution. Rationality implies an awareness of your own situation in the world, and your capacity to perform the actions necessary to deal with this. For anarchists, humans have an unlimited capacity to regulate their own lives. There is no knowledge that is unattainable and no problems that cannot be overcome. For anarcho-capitalists, this will be seen in a completely self-regulating free market.

Collectivist anarchists point to the *nurture* not *nature* debate, arguing that humans are essentially cooperative and social beings. They hold that once free from the influence of oppressive ideas and institutions, people will spontaneously combine to live and work together in a non-competitive fashion. This is seen in the different models of mutualism, anarcho-communism and anarcho-syndicalism.

Whatever their different views, for all types of anarchist Utopia is not only possible but necessary. It is the possibility of a better world that keeps humans afloat in a sea of misery.

Political practice

As anarchists believe that parliamentary democracy is a sham, they reject conventional political means to change society. Some attempt to change society in a revolutionary manner. Others attempt to create islands of anarchism within existing society.

content guidance

Such attempts often follow the principles of mutualism. This was first systematically formulated by Pierre Proudhon. The term had been used earlier, by Charles Fourier (1772–1837) in the 1820s, but not in the same sense. It is a view of how production might be organised in an anarchist society.

Proudhon attacked property as the result of coercion and theft. He contrasted this with possession. Here producers have the right to possess the outcome of their labour, and the right to possess in order to use necessary means (tools or land). This is not a capitalist property right of exclusive ownership and use. For Proudhon, this was the only way in which a viable society could exist. A society built on capitalist property rights would inevitably impoverish and destroy the majority of the population.

He recognised that some free association of producers beyond the family unit would be necessary. Modern industrial production demands this. For these units he advocated a system of democratic associations of workers. These would be free-standing bodies, with no outside social control. Proudhon's hostility to the state would permit no form of social regulation of production. The workers would have an absolute right to an equal share of the output of their enterprise.

Proudhon saw credit as being organised on the same basis as production. Free individuals would band together to provide a source of mutual credit to each other. This concept has influenced the contemporary credit unions in the UK, where members can draw on mutual funds.

Mutualism has influenced other contemporary activities. There have been numerous attempts to establish workers cooperatives on something approaching mutualist lines. The most long lasting and successful has been the Mondragon Cooperative in Spain. Most attempts have not survived for long. Local exchange trading systems (LETS) are another form of mutual credit, with no monetary element. Credit is earned by an activity, and is drawn on in the form of another activity.

In such ways, mutualism has proved to be one of the most attractive of anarchist principles. It is an expression that human nature is, among other things, about social solidarity.

Other anarchists have attempted to overthrow the state using revolutionary violence. The pre-1914 assassinations of ruling-class figures were intended to catalyse opposition from the masses. In this they signally failed. More effective were the attempts by anarcho-communists and anarcho-syndicalists to challenge the state through organised working-class action.

In the USA, this inspired the activities of the Industrial Workers of the World (IWW or 'Wobblies'). The IWW organised unskilled (often immigrant) labour to participate in a series of violent confrontations with employers and the police.

The period of revolution after the First World War gave anarcho-syndicalists their best chance. In Italy, at the end of the *Biennio Rosso* (the two red years) of 1919–21, the anarcho-syndicalists of the USI federation achieved a position of dominant influence in north-Italian industry in September 1921. They launched a revolutionary general strike occupying the factories. After a week, when capitalism and the state showed no sign of imminent collapse, the USI was forced to request the main trade-union federation, the CGI (dominated by reformist socialists), to vote on having a workers' revolution. This was (narrowly) rejected; the factory occupations collapsed, and with them the influence of the USI.

In the Catalonia region of Spain, the anarcho-syndicalist trade-union federation, the CNT, became the dominant force in the period 1915–36. When General Franco launched his military revolt against the democratically elected Popular Front government in July 1936, CNT militias were instrumental in defeating the rebels in Barcelona.

On that day, the main CNT leaders met with the liberal President of the Generalitat, the Catalonian regional government. He offered to hand over all power to them. This offer threw the leadership into a crisis. Later that day they agreed to decline his offer. The majority argued that to accept in conditions of civil war would mean imposing their form of libertarian communism on areas that did not yet support them. This would mean a form of dictatorship. For anarchists, this was impossible.

Therefore, they handed back power to the Generalitat (which, of course, the President had anticipated), and to the Popular Front government of evolutionary socialists with its supporters in the Communist Party. Despite significant success in experiments in running enterprises on a collective manner on syndicalist principles, within a year the CNT had been suppressed by the Popular Front government over the issue of incorporating its militias into the regular army.

Many people conclude that these two instances, at the moment of the anarcho-syndicalists' greatest influence, reveal the main reasons why anarchism has had such limited success in practical application. Their view of the state led them to either underestimate (Italy) or overestimate (Spain) the problems in taking power and transforming society. In both cases, the consequences were the victory of their bitterest enemies: Mussolini and Franco.

Individualist anarchism

Individualist anarchism stems from the anarchist view of human nature. It is another product of the Enlightenment emphasis on the individual and rationality. In this sense, it is an extreme form of liberalism.

Egoism is the belief that it is morally right to do what is in your own self-interest. It is often linked to the ideas of the German philosopher Max Stirner. At one time in the 1840s he was associated with the radical young Hegelian group of philosophers. Stirner's ideas were a response to the crude authoritarianism of the Prussian monarchy. He argued that all religions and ideologies — especially those of the Prussian state — were empty and meaningless. Only the individual has meaning, and all activity should be directed towards nurturing the individual.

Rational egoism is the idea that it is the core of rationality to act in your own self-interest. This version leant itself to the free-market aspects of economic liberalism, and then to what became known as libertarianism. It is no surprise, then, that the most influential theoretician for this idea was Ayn Rand. She termed her approach 'objectivism'.

Libertarians, like all anarchists, hold that *any* state authority is oppressive because it is a restraint on the free exercise of rational decision-making by the individual. Social relations should only be regulated by freely made contracts between individuals. Private property is central to this ideology, and its application to society has produced the sub-variant of anarcho-capitalism.

Anarcho-capitalism is a view of society, the economy and the state. It extends the idea of free-market liberalism to its furthest extent. Here, the market can fulfil all of the functions that Adam Smith allocated to the state. In line with mainstream anarchism, anarcho-capitalists argue that the state must be an oppressive force.

The term was coined by the economist Murray Rothbard (1926–95). He arrived at this position via association with the Austrian school, free-market economist von Mises and later with Ayn Rand. Unlike other anarchists, this theory embraces the exclusive nature of private property. The liberty of rational individuals can only be guaranteed by the absence of restraints on their ability to enjoy their property. Therefore, there can be *no* intervention or regulation by the state. Since this means that there can be no taxation, it means that there can be no state.

All residual state functions noted by Smith (law and order, justice, and defence) could be carried out by individual corporations. These would compete with each other to provide these services, on the basis of contracts agreed with citizens to give a sense of order. There would be a voluntarily agreed legal code, based on individual sovereignty, which courts would follow. Corporations would consist of the pooled capital of individuals, with limited liability. It would be possible to be a wage earner through contracts with these corporations.

Robert Nozick (1938–2002) was another American academic philosopher in this tradition. He advocated a free exchange of goods without any intervention or regulation by the state. This could then justify inequalities in society. For Nozick, the primacy of the rational individual meant that property rights were essential. Any violation of these would undermine natural rights and natural law.

Despite their similarities, there are significant differences between free-market liberalism and individualist anarchism. Unlike anarchists, liberals do believe in the necessity for some state and for limited constitutional government. Not everything can be left to the market.

Collectivist anarchism

Collectivist anarchism is a view of an ideal society and economy. It deviates from classical anarchism in that it has a central class aspect. This conflicts with the fundamentalist anarchist view of individualism. It shares a similar view of human nature as socialism. Humans are naturally social beings, who spontaneously cooperate with each other. There are two principal interpretations: anarcho-communism and anarcho-syndicalism.

Like other anarchists, anarcho-communists are absolutely hostile to the state. They advocate its total destruction, along with private property and capitalism. Anarcho-communism merged with modern industrial society in Western Europe after 1860. One its most important theorists was the Russian Peter Kropotkin (1842–1921). He argued that private property should be expropriated by the people, and distributed according to need.

Money and the wages system would be abolished on the road to abolishing social classes. Production would be carried out through voluntary associations, as in other anarchist traditions. There would be no form of collective ownership — producers would only have the right to use productive assets. There would be no form of market, as this would create inequalities which would lead to the re-emergence of classes and a new state.

All these are perfectly compatible with mainline communism. The single difference is the complete opposition to any form of state. Anarcho-communists are perfectly orthodox anarchists on this point. Any form of state will be oppressive, even (or especially) a revolutionary one.

Anarcho-communism tended to gain its greatest support in areas where industry was dominated by small-scale workshop production. These always had a high proportion of literate, self-educated, skilled workers. One example was the Jura Mountain area of France, where the largest trade was watch and clock making. There were also a large number of printers among the anarcho-communists.

Such people were attracted to anarcho-communism because it is comparatively easy to visualise how an anarcho-communist society could be created in their workplaces. In such enterprises, everyone knows each other and is aware of every stage of the production process (even if they are not skilled in more than one stage). In such conditions it is easy to conceive of everyone having a say in the operation of the enterprise. Before 1939 such small-scale enterprises were common in France, Italy and Spain, countries where anarcho-communism had its greatest support.

This explains how anarcho-communism had its greatest influence in Catalonia during the first year of the Spanish Civil War (1936–37). All the features that encouraged its growth had been present for many decades. Its fate here was linked with that of the CNT trade-union federation, which was dominated by the related tradition of anarcho-syndicalism (see below).

Anarcho-communist groups still exist in the UK and many other countries, but now have marginal ideological influence. The conditions which encouraged wide support have themselves become marginal. However, many of its principles have both had influence on, and re-emerged in, various forms of 'green' ideology (see the Unit Guide for Unit 4).

Anarcho-syndicalism is another class-based version of anarchism. It differs from anarcho-communism in that it has a clear and unique idea of the form of organisation that will be the agent of revolutionary change in society. This will also become the basic form of organisation in the new, free, classless society. That organisation is the trade union (syndicat is the French word for trade union).

Anarcho-syndicalism shares the anarchist belief in the rational individual, and a hatred of the state, capitalism and private property. It also wishes to abolish the wages system. It emerged as many anarchists joined trade unions in the last quarter of the nineteenth century. They saw the unions as truly voluntary, democratic and supportive organisations. This led many anarchists to conclude that these were unlike any other organisations in existing society. By their nature they were against private property and the state. They were created, controlled and funded by their members, and functioned as weapons against capitalism and the state.

Thus syndicalism developed into revolutionary trade unionism. Strike action would go beyond limited actions to improve wages and conditions. It could and should be used to bring down the state and capitalist society. By 1906, syndicalists had seized control of the French trade-union federation, the CGT. In their *Amiens Programme*, they set out a strategy of accelerated confrontation that would lead to a revolutionary general strike. They calculated that since capitalist society existed on the expropriation of the product of the labour of the working class, such an action would lead to the swift collapse of capitalism and the state.

In this strategy they rejected not only parliamentary democracy but *all* forms of politics. In this respect they were opposed to revolutionary socialists. They argued that politics was irrelevant and a distraction to the real working-class struggle. The general strike would finish off capitalism.

Since like all anarchists they were bitterly hostile to any form of state, this neatly evaded any need for a revolutionary state. The basis of capitalism having been expropriated in the strike, no counter-revolution would be possible. The unions would become the basis of the new society, organising both production and distribution of goods. No state would be necessary to carry out any function, because the unions would execute these.

Syndicalism rapidly became influential in much of Western Europe, especially in France, Italy and Spain. In the UK it had considerable influence over trade-union militants during the 'period of discontent', the era of militant mass strikes of 1910–14. During the First World War it inspired the Shop Stewards' Movement in industry. Syndicalism's great moment came with the victory of the CNT in Barcelona in 1936. As described above, this was swiftly followed by its eclipse. After temporarily recovering some influence in the industrial unrest in Western Europe in the early 1970s, its influence is limited to small groups of supporters.

Questions
&
Answers

This section of the book looks at a range of answers to the type of questions that you will face in your Unit 3 examination. It is divided into two content areas: short-answer questions in Section A and essay questions in Section B. Within each of these sections there are two sample answers for each of the ideologies. One of these is an A-grade and the other is a C-grade answer.

None of the answers is perfect. Each represents one way of approaching the question, with an indication of the grade that it might achieve.

Immediately after the question, before the student answer, you will find an examiner's advice section. This outlines the focus and scope of the question. Following each answer there is an 'Examiner's comment' (indicated by the symbol 🖉), which deals with the main strengths and weaknesses of the answer. In the essay-question answers you will also find shorter comments interspersed throughout the answer. These commentaries give you an indication of what is required to achieve an A-grade answer, and help you to become familiar with the three assessment objectives mentioned in the Introduction of this guide.

This book is intended to help you to develop your skills and capabilities. It is better to attempt the questions *first,* and then read the student answers and the comments. You can then review your work in the light of these. The student answers are *not* model answers to be memorised and then repeated word for word in the examination. You are unlikely to be faced with these specific questions and there is always more than one way in which a comprehensive answer can be given to any question.

Section A

*In this section you must answer **three** questions from a choice of five. There will be at least one question on each of the four ideologies covered in this guide.*

These questions are directed at one of the concepts discussed in the Content Guidance section. It is recommended that you spend no longer than 15 minutes on each question.

Remember that there are 5 marks for AO1 (knowledge), 7 marks for AO2 (analysis and evaluation) and 3 marks for AO3 (communication).

■ ■ ■

Liberalism

On what grounds have liberals raised concerns about democracy? (15 marks)

It is important to cite a range of reasons (i.e. two or more) for this answer. Remember that this is not a 'for and against' question. You only need to explain why some liberals have had concerns about democracy.

■ ■ ■

A-grade answer

In the past, liberals have raised concerns about democracy. It is viewed that liberals fear that democracy may not work for a number of reasons that this answer will discuss.

Early liberals such as Thomas Jefferson feared that democracy would lead to the tyranny of the majority against legitimate minority groups. This has happened in examples such as Northern Ireland, where the Catholic minority was oppressed by the Protestant majority.

John Stuart Mill recognised that democracy could cause concerns where an uneducated electorate could make ill-informed decisions on government policy that may focus on short-term whims rather than rational planning.

An uneducated electorate could also be easily swayed by charismatic individuals who could, with electoral support, become tyrannical dictators. An example of this happening was the rise and support of Mussolini by the peasant farmers of Italy.

Concerns about democracy could also be raised by some liberals when trying to pursue liberal ideological goals, such as tolerance, freedom, natural rights and rationalist policies, when opposed by a less ideologically driven electorate. What

liberal philosophers may have wanted may not be what the majority of the people wanted.

✐ The four main paragraphs all directly address the question, even though the introduction should state why liberals have concerns about democracy.

Despite being short, each paragraph contributes a new point and is credit worthy. The references to Jefferson and Mill are relevant and effective. Each point would benefit from being slightly more extensive, for instance the point about an uneducated electorate could have been supported by a reference to Robert Lowe and the 1867 Reform Act. The interesting point raised in the final paragraph would be improved by a specific reference.

For the level of knowledge demonstrated by this response, the candidate would receive 4 marks out of the 5 AO1 marks available for knowledge and understanding.

For the quality of analysis, the candidate would receive 6 marks out of the 7 AO2 marks available for analysis and evaluation of political information.

For the quality of argument developed through the answer, the examiner would award 2 marks out of the 3 AO3 marks available for constructing and communicating coherent arguments. In total, this answer would receive 12 marks.

■ ■ ■

C-grade answer

Liberals chose democracy as a system of government as it is seen as the lesser of two evils. As Churchill put it 'democracy is the worst form of government, except all other forms'. This shows that even though democracy represents the will and the sovereignty of the people, liberals still have major concerns about it.

One concern liberals have about democracy is that majority rule may prevail. This idea was brought about by the French liberal Alexis de Tocqueville in the form of the 'tyranny of the majority'. As democracy works on the basis that 51% is a majority, large unrepresented minorities are formed and this is what liberals fear. This would infringe against liberal interest and liberty and in turn question the idea of consent legitimising government. De Tocqueville also said that democracy produced 'dull conformism' rather than individualism.

Liberals are also worried that many voters are uneducated people who are easy to deceive. This could lead to 'mob rule', which was described by the philosopher Plato. Clever and unscrupulous politicians could manipulate people to get themselves elected and then set up oppressive governments, like the Nazis did in Germany.

e This answer does mention three relevant issues, but fails to develop them all suffi-ciently to provide a comprehensive response to the question. The introduction does not take the answer forward, as the statement in its final sentence does not follow from the Churchill quote.

The second paragraph makes the 'tyranny of the majority' point with some development, and an undeveloped 'dull conformity' point in the final sentence. This should have been developed in a separate paragraph, with reference to the liberal emphasis on the importance of the development of individual potential.

The final paragraph gives the 'mob-rule' argument, although the Nazi example is not the most accurate one to use here (the Nazis were losing electoral support when they came to power). A reference to the liberal argument against referendums as a means of manipulation by opportunist demagogues would have been relevant, for instance.

For level of knowledge, the candidate would receive 3 marks. For the quality of analysis, the candidate would receive 4 marks. For the quality of argument developed through the answer, the candidate would receive 2 marks. In total, this answer would receive 9 out of the 15 marks available.

Question 2

Conservatism

Distinguish between the liberal New Right and the conservative New Right.

(15 marks)

📝 It is important to balance this answer between both interpretations. You need to focus on those aspects where they differ, especially on human nature, society and the state. You should give examples of both to illustrate and support your arguments.

■ ■ ■

A-grade answer

The liberal New Right, or neo-liberalism, is largely influenced by the ideas of Adam Smith. The liberal New Right has been influenced by classical liberal economics. It therefore stresses the need for a self-regulating market which is free from government interference. The liberal New Right therefore puts its faith not in government but in the individual and the market.

Neo-liberalism emerged during the 1970s, directly challenging the Keynsian social democracy which was prominent at the time. Its aim is to halt and even reverse the tendency towards big government, which has characterised the second half of the twentieth century, and neo-liberals would point to the centrally planned economies of the USSR and Eastern Europe to demonstrate the inefficiency of government intervention in the economy. Neo-liberals also stress negative freedom; Nozick, for example, described all policies of welfare and redistribution as 'organised theft'.

The conservative New Right stresses social authoritarianism. Its main concerns are regarding law and order, public morality and national identity. Neo-conservatives stress the need for a strong state because they believe that the cult of the individual and the spread of permissive values has undermined authority and weakened social cohesion. Neo-conservatives also fear moral pluralism, which can also lead to the choosing of immoral or evil views. For some neo-conservatives, issues such as abortion, homosexuality and pornography have all been castigated as morally bad.

Neo-conservatives also seek to strengthen national identity. In the UK this has been evident in the rise of Euroscepticism and a fear of multiculturalism, while in the USA this has been evident in the 'war on terror' in the desire to resist Islamic fundamentalism.

Andrew Gamble thus described Thatcherism as the commitment to 'the free economy and the strong state'. In some respects, the two apparently contrasting traditions complement each other because the neo-conservative emphasis on strict punishments and a strong state helps to counter the social pressures unleashed by the neo-liberal insistence upon economic liberalism.

This candidate shows a sophisticated grasp of all aspects of the New Right. In addition, the essay is written with a lucid use of political terminology and is well organised.

The introduction gives defining characteristics of the liberal New Right, with its ideological point of origin. This will enable a clear distinction to be made with the conservative New Right later in the answer.

There is a good balance in covering both sides of the New Right, and appropriate and useful examples are given from the initial influence of Adam Smith to the nature of neo-liberalism developed in the 1970s. Neo-conservatism is well developed in its authoritarian and nationalist aspects. While there is a lack of explicit points of distinction during the main discussion, the conclusion is a model of how to make a judgement for these questions, using Gamble's classic summary of the New Right.

For the level of knowledge, the candidate would receive 4 marks. For the quality of analysis, the candidate would receive 7 marks. For the quality of argument developed through the answer, the candidate would receive 3 marks. A total of 14 marks would be awarded for this answer.

■ ■ ■

C-grade answer

The liberal New Right, also known as neo-liberalism, subscribes to traditional free-market values that encourage capitalism and profit, as well as individualism in society. The conservative New Right, on the other hand, follows a more traditional conservative view.

The conservative New Right preaches authority from above, believing that humans are irrational and security-seeking and therefore require authority imposed on them, because they are unaware of what is good for them.

This form of conservatism follows a traditional view, believing in an organic society and holding faith with institutions such as the family.

While the liberal New Right is liberal economically, the conservative New Right does not follow this line. The conservative New Right sees the family as the basis for everything: it is a starting point for authority for children, and teaches them respect, and is also a method of sustaining security. Conservative New Rightists believe humans to be fundamentally flawed.

The view on human nature is one of the biggest distinguishing factors between the liberal and conservative New Right. For example, the liberal belief is that humans are rational and capable of development, while the conservative view is one of imperfection: humans are morally, psychologically and intellectually flawed.

The very different views regarding human nature also create differences in the type of state or government provided. The liberal New Right will follow a classical liberal or libertarian line — one of minimal intervention — whereas the conservative New Right believes in a strong state or government that will guarantee stability and security. The conservative New Right sees humans as irrational and driven by impulses such as greed, lust and envy, and so inclined to commit crimes. A strong social stance is needed to curb this.

However, both the liberal and conservative New Right see property as an important requirement, but for different reasons. While the liberal New Right sees property ownership as the result of hard work (the fruits of one's labour), the conservative New Right feels it is necessary to engender stability and social security. Proponents also believe that it fosters respect, because those with houses are less likely to damage other people's property. For conservatives, it is an extension of one's personality.

In conclusion, the liberal New Right is very close to liberalism, while the conservative New Right strengthens traditional Victorian values.

e This is a classic example of an unbalanced answer. Everything written is accurate, but there is too much on the issue of human nature, and in particular the conservative view. The neo-liberal view on the importance of the free market is mentioned but hardly developed. Since the free market is the defining aspect of neo-liberalism, this is a serious omission. There should have been some reference to the revived influence of the ideas of Adam Smith in the context of the 1970s and his influence on contemporary thinkers such as Nozick or Friedman. Therefore, this a partial answer, albeit with the one aspect well developed.

For the level of knowledge, the candidate would receive 3 marks. For the quality of analysis, the candidate would receive 4 marks. For the quality of argument, the candidate would receive 2 marks. This answer would receive a total of 9 marks.

Socialism

Why do socialists support collectivism, and how have they done it? (15 marks)

🖉 This is a two-part question, and the answer should be balanced to reflect this. There should be a range of points given to both parts, ideally with at least one drawn from each of the traditions — evolutionary and revolutionary socialism.

■ ■ ■

A-grade answer

Socialists support collectivism for moral and practical reasons. Morally, this support arises from their view of human nature. They believe that people are naturally social beings. Left to themselves, they cooperate with each other for the common good. Competition is an unnatural condition, imposed on people by the ruling class for its own benefit. Collectivism strengthens these natural social bonds.

Collectivism is also more efficient than individualism and competitiveness. More is achieved by working together than by working against others. Economic competition leads to wasteful duplication of resources, and leads to the overproduction of similar versions of the same product. Collectivism implies planning the most efficient use of resources for the benefit of the whole community.

Socialists have promoted collectivism in a number of ways. One of the first ways was through trade unions — workers organised together to bargain for higher wages and to improve their working conditions. Unions also protect and promote the general interest of the working class. In many countries they have campaigned to extend democracy and have opposed dictatorships.

Unions have also promoted retail cooperatives to give workers cheap goods and food. The have also supported workers cooperatives to give workers the ability to control their own workplaces and keep all the income from their work.

Socialists have promoted social-welfare systems and redistribution of income through taxing wealth. These policies were intended to strengthen social solidarity by showing a collective responsibility for the wellbeing of all sections of society.

🖉 This is a well-balanced answer that addresses both the 'why' and 'how' aspects of the question. It clearly distinguishes two 'why' arguments (the social nature of human beings and the efficiency of collaboration) and develops both. The answer also gives three 'how' points (trade unions, cooperatives and social welfare), although these are not as clearly explained as those for 'why'. For instance, the paragraph on cooperatives could have mentioned how they made cheap and unadulterated food available to the working class, which links with the 'why' argument of efficiency. A similar development could have been made for the last point on social welfare — providing a healthier and more educated workforce.

3

question

For the level of knowledge demonstrated by this response, the candidate would receive 4 marks. For the quality of analysis, the candidate would receive 6 marks. For the quality of argument developed through the answer, the candidate would receive 2 marks. A total of 12 marks would be awarded for this answer.

■ ■ ■

C-grade answer

Socialists support collectivism because they believe in the core principles of community, cooperation and equality.

They believe that human beings are sociable creatures not naturally self-serving, and that we achieved society through mutual aid. Some examples of collectivism are found in the Stalin era (merging of farms), as there was no need for property. Efficiency was promoted through the merging of the farms into communities. This collectivism also ties in with the socialist view of equality, that all men are equal, and eliminates the traditional hierarchical structures of work, in line with the socialist view of no property, equality, cooperation and the community. Marx said in the closing of the Communist manifesto: 'Workers of the world, unite.'

Self-sufficient communes sprang up in the 1960s and 1970s as a product of socialism. They were based on collectivist principles and acted as a promotion for collectivism. Some governments, such as the UK Labour governments, supported collectivism through nationalisation.

There is a brief but accurate statement in the introduction answering the 'why' aspect, although it is underdeveloped. More explanation of the socialist view of human nature (being social and collaborative) would be helpful.

The candidate then falls into a common trap of identifying 'collectivism' with 'collectivisation'. Most of the answer to 'how' is taken up with this. It is accurate, but limited. More examples, such as of trade unions and cooperatives, would have been useful, as they would have extended the range of the answer.

Most of the final paragraph is a dubious proposition, apart from the final sentence on nationalisation, which needs to be developed. However, the answer does address both parts of the question with valid material, even though it is unbalanced and brief.

For the level of knowledge demonstrated by this response, the candidate would receive 2 marks. For quality of analysis, the candidate would receive 4 marks. For the quality of argument developed through the answer, the candidate would receive 2 marks. A total of 8 marks would be awarded for this answer.

Anarchism

Why have anarchists believed that the state is unnecessary? (15 marks)

e It is vital to remember that the question uses the word 'unnecessary'. It does not ask why anarchists think that the state is 'undesirable' or 'evil'. Your answer should concentrate on the positive aspects of human nature, such as rationality and cooperation, that make any state unnecessary.

■ ■ ■

A-grade answer

Anarchists believe the state is unnecessary because all major aspects of anarchism optimistically believe that humans are naturally rational and desire to be free individuals.

Anarcho-capitalism is the extreme liberal view that the economic structure should be a totally unregulated free market. It can and should operate by the 'invisible hand' of the laws of supply and demand. This will stop the system failing. There is no need for a state, as the system will operate perfectly well without one, and individuals will cooperate to make it do so through their enlightened self-interest. It will produce a stable and just society.

On the other hand, anarcho-communists believe the state is unnecessary because it can be replaced by mutualism, the idea of 'mutual aid' put forward by Kropotkin. Because this type of anarchism sees humans as social, cooperative and gregarious creatures, they think that people will use the 'labour for labour' exchange as an economic system. They do not need a state to achieve these aims, as human society has evolved naturally through cooperation. Anarcho-syndicalists believe that there is no need for a state because the functions of a society can be carried out through trade unions. They argue that these democratic bodies can organise all functions of production and distribution in society.

So both sides see no need for a state because of their view of human nature. Because of this, peace and prosperity will emerge spontaneously. Humans will naturally avoid conflict and violence. They do not need a state to keep law and order.

e This is a balanced answer that addresses the question asked. It begins with a clear definition of the key reason why anarchists consider the state to be unnecessary: human nature. It avoids the danger of drifting into explaining why anarchists think that the state is undesirable.

It then provides three different ways of interpretation from major aspects of anarchist thought: anarcho-capitalism, anarcho-communism and anarcho-syndicalism. Each of these interpretations is explained, although they could be

supported by a brief example, for example the anarcho-capitalist belief that police functions could be put out to tender by private enterprise.

For level of knowledge, the candidate would receive 4 marks. For quality of analysis, the candidate would receive 6 marks. For quality of argument, the candidate would receive 2 marks. A total of 12 marks would be awarded for this answer.

■ ■ ■

C-grade answer

While conservatives believe that the state protects, and liberals view it as a necessary evil, anarchists reject both points of view and deem the state to be an unnecessary evil.

They believe that the purpose of the state is to take away the individual's freedom. Anarchists believe that people can live peaceably together without laws. Some, such as anarcho-communists, believe that humans are social animals and will live together happily and for mutual benefit. Anti-social behaviour is only caused by being brought up in a capitalist environment.

Anarchists believe that humans will live happily together because of their basic human nature. Capitalist anarchists believe that the free market will function well automatically without any state interference. The state conflicts with this due to its need to organise and construct laws. Laws conflict with the supreme rights of individuals by creating barriers to the individuals' right to act freely.

An anarchist will argue that the state is not needed as people will agree to cooperate in a 'state of nature'. Violence and disorder is produced by the state, not by people.

📝 This is an example of an answer which is confused about what is being asked. Immediately in the introduction it falls into the trap of confusing necessity and desirability. This sends the answer in the wrong direction. It then veers between addressing the issue of necessity (which was asked) and desirability (which was not), which produces a disjointed response. However, it does mention the core point of human nature, although it fails to refer to the central issue of human rationality.

Two different anarchist views are mentioned, but only briefly. The anarcho-communist view requires more development regarding how humans might live together, and the anarcho-capitalist view is not supported by a specific example.

For level of knowledge, the candidate would receive 2 marks. For quality of analysis, the candidate would receive 4 marks. For quality of argument, the candidate would receive 2 marks. This answer would receive 8 marks in total.

Question 5

Section B

*In Section B, you must answer **one** question from a choice of three. This means that one of the ideologies will not have an essay question set in each examination. It is important to understand that there is no set rotation for specific ideologies to appear in this section. You must prepare for the examination on the basis that **any** three could appear.*

The questions in this section examine major issues concerned with the ideologies. They will require you to discuss differences and similarities between the various versions of the ideologies and come to a reasoned judgement on the question asked.

Remember, the marks for essays are:
- *AO1 = 12*
- *AO2 = 24 (including 12 for synopticity)*
- *AO3 = 9*
  Total = 45

■ ■ ■

Liberalism

Analyse similarities and differences between classical liberalism and modern liberalism. (45 marks)

 This question openly requires a balanced approach. You should examine similarities on key issues of the individual, human rights and rationality and then highlight and explain the differences over definitions of freedom and the approach to the economy and the state. You should also discuss any recent movements in opinion among both traditions and then make a judgement about the extent of the differences and similarities.

■ ■ ■

A-grade answer

Although there clearly are many differences between classical and modern liberals, they still both hold a fundamental commitment to the importance of individual freedom and to the principles of individualism. Both classical and modern liberals see individualism as their key value. However, they differ in their interpretation of the principle.

Classical liberals believe in egotistical individualism, where each individual is independent and self-reliant. Society is therefore 'atomised', meaning it is simply a collection of individuals who seek advancement only for themselves.

question

Modern liberals still hold to the basis of this thought, but have adapted it to modern conditions. They believe in developmental individualism. This is where individuals are given a certain amount of protection from the state in order that they have the optimum conditions to flourish and develop to their full potential. Society is therefore no longer seen as atomised and instead modern liberals hold a more altruistic approach, where individuals are somewhat self-reliant but also care for the wellbeing of others. The approach is not as selfish as that of classical liberals.

Although modern liberals differ from the classical liberals in that they see a greater need for state intervention to ensure adequate development of the individual, both wings of liberalism hold an underlying fear of the state. Both wings see the potential for the state to corrupt the individual's freedom, which is the key principle of individualism.

Classical liberals see this in the extent to which this involves negative freedom. This involves total freedom for the individual, without any restrictions. Modern liberals practise positive freedom where, as previously stated, the state provides a limited level of inputs and restrictions. This, however, is merely to encourage individuals to fulfil their potential and to blossom and flourish.

The fear of the state is clear through the liberals' view of the economy too. Classical liberals do, however, hold a different view of the economy to the modern wing.

Classical liberals believe in Adam Smith's theory of the free-market economy. They believe that the government should not intervene in the workings of the economy. Instead they see that the market should be run by an 'invisible hand'. This is the idea of laissez-faire economics, which clearly backs up the liberals' fear of the state.

Modern liberals, however, have seen the benefits of a post-capitalist economy to generate wealth. Following the postwar consensus, Keynes and Beveridge both rejected the idea of the free market and embraced the notion that a mixed economy would be more beneficial to society. Clearly, this differs from the classical liberal view of the economy, but still it complements the theme of a fear of the state as they do not encourage full state control, only a mixed economy.

Classical liberals also believe that the state should merely act as a 'safety net' when delivering welfare. The role of the state has been described as being that of a 'nightwatchman'. The modern liberals believe that welfare is a more important aspect of society than the classical liberals. They see the need to protect the disadvantaged, but again, the role of the state in delivering this welfare ought to be limited.

Consequently, the underlying principles of individualism and fearing the state are similar to both wings of the liberal ideology. However, the extent of the commitment to these differs between the classical and modern liberals.

⊘ This answer addresses the demands of the question. It covers the two different concepts of freedom and then looks at the divergence in views on economic regulation. The introduction clearly identifies individualism as the key to liberal thought, leading on to discussion of the two different views.

The discussion on individualism is unbalanced. The paragraph on the classical view should have included reference to the importance of rationality and to human rights. On the other hand, the paragraph on the modern liberal view is good, offering a well-developed evaluation of the core arguments.

Unfortunately, the discussion on the state is not well organised since it is divided in two, separated by the section of the differing views on the economy. Its effectiveness and clarity is greatly reduced by this.

The section on the economy is accurate, but should explain why modern liberals think that state regulation is effective, for example Keynes' view that the free market can be dysfunctional, as in 1929–31. The candidate would have done better to use Beveridge in the section on developmental individualism.

The conclusion does not add anything to the answer and simply reiterates the main points of the essay. However, overall the answer does provide a good understanding and analysis of the key issues (even if uneven). It is an example of how you do not have to produce a perfect answer to achieve an A grade.

Marks
AO1 = 9
AO2 = 9 + 8 (for synopticity)
AO3 = 7
Total = 33

■ ■ ■

C-grade answer

Classical liberalism and modern liberalism have some differences between them, but some ideas remain the same.

The overriding principle that has remained the same between both kinds of liberals is the supreme importance of the individual over any social group. They both see this as the fundamental basis of liberalism and both aim to uphold individuals' rights and freedom, as long as these do not infringe on the rights of other individuals. They do, however, differ about how they wish to protect the individual.

Classical liberals see the state as a necessary evil and only there to protect the rights of individuals and nothing else. Modern liberals, however, believe that some people do need help because they are less able. This is why they advocate the need for a bigger state and why the 'welfare state' case was made — so people who are less able can get benefits and welfare in order to enhance self-development.

Classical liberals hold a firm belief in the free market and follow it ideologically. This is because it promotes competition, which is important because they see competition as being natural and it will only help with reaching your full potential. They feel that a person should do whatever he or she feels is necessary to maximise profits. For example, a business should be able to outsource in order to find the cheapest labour, such as call-centres moving to Asia because labour is cheaper. Therefore, they are maximising their profits as much as they can, which is fine because it is natural to be greedy.

Modern liberals also support the free-market ideas of Adam Smith, but they realise their limitations, which is why they do not follow them so closely as do classical liberals. They realise that it is necessary for the state to intervene in times of crisis so that individual freedom is maintained. This is why they advocate the need for a bigger state, because sometimes there are factors outside individuals' control which will reduce their freedom and infringe on their rights, such as famines and economic crises.

Both classical and modern liberals believe in toleration and pluralism. They believe that they go hand in hand. Toleration is important because it guarantees that every individual can have their own beliefs. This is why liberals use the saying of Voltaire: 'I detest what you say but I defend to the death your right to say it.' If you don't agree with what someone says or believes in you should still allow them to express it. This is where the idea of pluralism comes in. Both types of liberal support pluralism because it leads to competition, which is natural and important in enhancing self-development and allowing people to reach their full potential. Without pluralism you will only get dull conformism, which is why they oppose censorship. This is because without pluralism you are infringing the rights of individuals and taking away their freedom to express themselves. Therefore, this would cripple the whole structure of liberalism.

Therefore, classical and modern liberals do have similarities and differences. They are similar in that they wish to promote individualism and they encourage pluralism and toleration. However, there are differences on what they say about the role of the state. Classical liberals favour a minimal state with little intervention, while modern liberals recognise the need for a bigger state because it can widen individual freedom and protect rights. Also, classical liberals follow the free-market ideas of Adam Smith almost religiously, while modern liberals are willing to accept that there are limitations to it. On the whole, there has been some evolution of ideas between classical and modern liberals, but the main principle of upholding individualism still remains a priority.

The answer does attempt the full range of the question, and there are some points of merit in each part of the answer. However, it is limited by a lack of clarity in a number of definitions and a failure to provide sufficient analysis. The introduction is inadequate and does not clearly define the issues contained in the question. The answer should have defined liberalism as a way of opening up the discussion required by the question.

In the first main paragraph, the core principle of the individual is clearly defined. The discussion on the state is too brief (classical liberals also argue the state has a duty to protect society from external attack) and not well expressed.

The paragraphs on the market have a general sense of the two positions, but again lack precision. The real debate is about the ability to obtain the most effective use of resources: the free market (classical liberals, following Smith) or government intervention (modern liberals).

The paragraph on toleration and pluralism is weak on the latter. Liberals support pluralism because in the modern world it is an essential support for individual liberty, not because it assists competition or prevents dull conformism. The paragraph ends with a correct statement, but one which is not the product of the preceding discussion.

The conclusion is not an evaluation of the discussion, but a repetition of the main points. Only the last sentence attempts evaluation, but with little effect.

Marks
AO1 = 6
AO2 = 6 + 6 (for synopticity)
AO3 = 5
Total = 23

Conservatism

To what extent are there tensions within conservatism over its support for the individual and its commitment to community? (45 marks)

📝 Here you need to contrast the differences between traditional and one-nation conservatism and the neo-liberal aspect of the New Right. The question specifically addresses views on human nature and on society. You must point out that there are tensions within the New Right — neo-conservatism has more in common with the other traditions on these aspects than it has with neo-liberalism.

■ ■ ■

A-grade answer

The tensions visible within conservatism are most clearly and simply highlighted by Gamble in *A Free Economy and a Strong State*. This implies a tension between choice and individualism, and social security and the community.

Paternalistic conservatives have always concerned themselves with matters of the community. Benjamin Disraeli outlined the issue when he wrote 'we are in danger of becoming two nations: the rich and the poor'. He committed himself to reducing this gap and acting on behalf of the community as a whole. Conservatism has taken this stance in order to preserve the position of the ruling class.

It is argued that if the lower end of society is content, then there is less chance of revolution. In addition to this, paternalistic conservatives cite *'noblesse oblige'* as a reason for concentrating on the community. This principle states that as they find themselves in positions of authority, the ruling classes must also meet obligations in terms of helping those without power.

Paternalists also believe in the rights of an individual to own property. This is because it is felt that a person is entitled to inherit property from previous generations. This elitist view places some value in the individual. However, traditionally conservatives and the paternalistic tradition have been concerned with the community more than the individual, and have taken a pragmatic approach to the economy, favouring any system that will work at a particular time.

New Right conservatives concern themselves with reversing the economic and moral decline that they see in society. This commits them to a strong state in order to reverse social decline. Margaret Thatcher saw the decline in moral values as a result of a breakdown in family values and advocated a return to 'Victorian values'. In this way she was considered to be neo-conservative and placed an emphasis on community. Neo-conservatism also places an emphasis on religion and its ability to provide security within society. The 'moral majority' campaign implemented by Reagan is such an example of the New Right's commitment to community.

questions & answers

The neo-liberal element focuses heavily on the individual in both a social and economic sense. *The Road to Serfdom*, written by von Hayek, critiques the intervention of the state and claims that it robs people of their self-reliance and creates a dependency culture. This clearly emphasises the tension within the New Right between individual liberty and the community.

Neo-liberals also favour individuals in terms of the economy. Friedman critiques the USSR and state intervention in the economy, concluding that intervention had a harmful effect. As a result, a belief in free-market capitalism is instilled in the New Right. Thatcher's commitment to this can be viewed when she claimed: 'There is no such thing as society.' This is in direct contrast to other New Right policies aimed at reversing social decline and further highlights tensions within conservatism.

In conclusion, paternalistic conservatives favour a commitment to the community and only hold individualism in high regard when viewing property ownership. Over that there is little tension within the ideology. However, the dogmatic approach to the economy of the New Right and Reagan's love of 'rugged individualism' suggest a leaning towards priority for the individual. However, a huge tension also exists within the New Right because of its commitment to reversing decline in the community. As a result, tensions exist within conservatism as a whole, between paternalists and the New Right, as well as within the two factions. This means that striking a balance between individualism and the community is a key issue for conservative ideology.

🖉 The problem with this answer is an imbalance in the treatment of traditional conservative viewpoints, since it omits any discussion on the theory of the organic society. Although the introduction is short, it does provide a clear structure for the essay, related to a major book on the issues.

The section on paternalism could benefit from a reference to the theory of organic society, which drives traditional conservatives to support 'community' in the form of the existing social structure. This could easily have been incorporated into the section on Disraeli and paternalism.

The last section is excellent, as it explains the core theories of the two sections of the New Right and the tensions between them. It shows useful examples (although Thatcher's famous quote is slightly out of context, since it was made in the context of a debate on welfare, not the economy).

The conclusion effectively evaluates the discussion in the main body of the essay, and provides the answer requested in the question by highlighting the tensions within conservative thought.

Marks
AO1 = 9
AO2 = 10 + 9 (for synopticity)
AO3 = 8
Total = 36

question 6

C-grade answer

An organic society can be considered a core principle of conservatism. The belief that all people and social groups should work together is founded and supported by many other core conservative principles. It is clear that despite the apparent individualistic approach adopted by many conservatives, it can be argued that a commitment to the collective, or an organic society, has created tensions within conservatism.

Traditional conservatives would strongly advocate an organic society, and would support the stability that it provides people. This attitude can be said to be prioritised above the interests of the individual.

Furthermore, one-nation conservatives draw heavily on the idea of an organic society and community in their ideas. The idea of the rich having duties and obligations threatens the individual in order to retain 'one nation'. Paternalistic conservatives such as Disraeli would argue that private property has to be infringed on. Taxes must be taken in order to raise the living standards of those who are least advantaged. Therefore, it can be argued that the commitment to the community has infringed on individual rights and as a result support for the individual has been undermined.

However, it can also be argued that one-nation conservatives retain strong support for the individual. Disraeli argued that helping the poor will in turn prevent social revolution. The prevention of revolution in fact benefits the individual and allows for continued prosperity.

New Right conservatives adopt a different approach to the community. Social libertarians argue for both economic and social liberty. By doing this they are placing great emphasis on the role of the individual. While not disputing the idea of an organic society, the promotion of economic liberty in particular highlights support for the individual. Therefore, within social libertarians there is little tension between support for the individual and commitment to the community.

Neo-conservatives also adopt the idea of economic liberty. Freedom from state intervention means that the individual is supported. Margaret Thatcher argued that: 'There is no such thing as society, only individuals and their families.' This shows a complete disregard for the community and an organic society. It is clear that Thatcher believed in the primacy of the individual within the workings of life and interactions with others.

Despite this, neo-conservatives do view morality as a social issue. Therefore it could be argued that support for community is inevitable as it is the task of the community to deal with social issues. Furthermore, they would advocate a strong role for law and order, which can be seen as support for the idea of commitment to the community. However, it can be argued that a strong society benefits individuals because they are protected from others and are allowed to continue to prosper.

Although it may appear that a commitment to the community outweighs support for the individual, it can clearly be seen that the adoption of such methods is merely exercised to benefit the individual. The solid hierarchical structure of the organic society benefits the individual in many ways. Therefore, although it is possible for tensions to occur over the means to which the individual is promoted, aims and results are the same, support for the individual is paramount.

⌦ This attempt to challenge the premise of the question is unsuccessful. It tries to reverse the normal approach: that the individualism of neo-liberalism causes tensions within conservatism. This is a difficult task and needs to be well argued to work.

The answer partly fails because the attempt to show traditional or one-nation attitudes towards the individual are extrapolated from possible practical impacts, rather than from the ideas themselves. The first section deals with impacts of ideas, not with any hostility to individualism as such. For instance, it misses out the traditional and one-nation view on the imperfection of human nature.

In the paragraph on the New Right, there is no support for the final sentence in the rest of the paragraph, and social libertarians certainly do see tension between the interests of the individual and of the community. They view this as threatening to individual freedom.

The answer is further undermined by the misunderstanding of social libertarian views. The argument is better when dealing with the New Right, although it places the Thatcher quote slightly out of context.

The final section on neo-conservatism is good, dealing with several core values of neo-conservatism, although the possibility that the Thatcher quote is more of a neo-liberal statement is not discussed.

Marks
AO1 = 8
AO2 = 5 + 6 (for synopticity)
AO3 = 6
Total = 25

Socialism

Why did socialists believe in gradualism, and why has gradualism failed?   (45 marks)

The first part of this question requires a discussion of the evolutionary socialist position. A comprehensive answer would deal with a range of arguments, such as the Fabian, revisionist Marxist and third-way positions. Reasons for failure could come from the orthodox Marxist and fundamentalist socialist viewpoints. This is one question when it is certainly possible to challenge the question and say that gradualism has not failed, but this needs to be carefully argued with clear supporting evidence.

■ ■ ■

A-grade answer

Early socialists in Western Europe took a revolutionary standpoint when deciding which means were the best with which to achieve socialism. However, with the introduction of the extension of the franchise, an increase in trade unions and the establishment of social democratic political parties, the 'oppressed' classes maintained that they could reach what they believed in via the ballot box, as opposed to violent revolution.

Socialists believed in what is known as 'the inevitability of gradualism', the idea that it is inevitable that socialist principles would eventually prosper. This was largely due to the extension of the franchise and eventually achieving universal suffrage. The concept of giving every person of a certain age the right to vote would mean that the opinion of the majority would prosper. The majority is the proletariat, the working class. The proletariat is largely socialist in belief, thus leading to the repeated election of social democratic parties. These parties would legislate to the benefit of the proletariat and implement laws to stop its exploitation, and so socialist principles would flourish as gradualism occurs. In theory it is possible to see why socialists believed in this; however, in practice gradualism was not realised.

As Western Europe became more technologically advanced, more skilled workers (as opposed to labourers) were required. In conjunction with the decline of coal mines and steelworks, the number of skilled workers surpassed the number of traditional manual workers (the stereotypical proletariat). Therefore, the majority of people were becoming middle class and their working conditions and lifestyle were vastly improving. The introduction of the divorce of ownership and control (which mainly occurred in public limited companies) meant that specialist managers were running the large companies instead of the owners (shareholders). The managers would therefore be less interested in profit maximising than they would be in maintaining a good public image and a happy workforce, thus the conditions for the working class improved.

As the majority of people were now becoming middle class, they would be less likely to identify and support socialist principles. Thus they might use universal suffrage to vote for a liberal or conservative party that might represent their views better. Therefore, there would be no possibility of domination by socialist parties.

When socialist parties do now get into power it is becoming increasingly difficult for them to legislate as much reform as they would like to. This is largely due to the fact that other institutions of power, for example the House of Lords, the courts and the police, tend to be middle class, with middle-class principles. They can dilute the governing party's power to make policy. The government also has to liaise with big business in order to obtain party funding and thus needs to keep business happy, as well as the proletariat. All of these factors have led to the supposed failure of gradualism.

This failure of gradualism has led many to believe in the 'death of socialism'. However, others would say that while gradualism may not have followed its designated path, it has transformed us all into socialists. Socialism, in Britain at least, is very much alive through the welfare state: the National Health Service, unemployment benefit and free education up to the age of eighteen. When the distribution of wealth has come so far and class barriers have nearly become eradicated, how would one say that gradualism has truly failed? Socialism itself may be considered dead, but the result of socialism is very much alive.

The essay succinctly covers all the required elements. The introduction clearly identifies the issue contained in the question and the origins of gradualism in terms of changes in socialist ideas.

The next section clearly sets out 'why' in terms of a revisionist Marxist analysis of the development of society. This section could be developed further with more explicit distinction between Fabian and revisionist Marxist ideas. However, this again shows that you do not need to write a perfect answer to achieve high marks. It is then followed by three paragraphs addressing 'failure'. The answer deals with the sociological reason for failure, and then the incorporation reason, both of which are well explained.

The excellent conclusion makes a reasoned case for challenging the assumption of the question. The fact that many might regard it as controversial does not reduce its credit-worthiness as an examination answer. Only the imbalance between belief and failure in this answer prevents it from gaining full marks.

Marks
AO1 = 10
AO2 = 10 + 11 (for synopticity)
AO3 = 9
Total = 40

C-grade answer

Evolutionary socialists believe in gradualism. They think that it is possible to change society 'bit by bit'. They can do this using parliamentary democracy. By getting a majority in parliament, a socialist government can introduce laws which will change society and introduce equality, the main socialist principle.

Socialist parties, especially the British Labour party, thought that they could use working-class votes to bring about change. In 1945 this seemed to work when the Labour Party won a big majority in the general election. They then tried to take over the 'commanding heights' of the economy by nationalising industries like coal and the railways. These were to be used for the benefit of the whole community, not just for private profit. They also tried to introduce equality throught the welfare state and the National Health Service. Other socialist parties in Western Europe did the same thing in the 1940s and 1950s.

Gradualism failed for several reasons. First, the working class declined in size. By the 1970s there were more and more white-collar workers who did not think of themselves as working class, but middle class. In the 1980s many of these began to vote Conservative when Margaret Thatcher tried to attract their votes with policies such as selling council houses and privatisation. Labour lost four elections in a row. It was only able to win elections when Tony Blair introduced New Labour and changed Clause 4 of the Party constitution to abandon nationalisation.

In the 1990s and 2000s, capitalism seemed to be able to deliver increasing living standards. Globalisation meant that workers could get more and more consumer goods at cheap prices. Many people could have cheap foreign holidays all over the world. In 1991 the old Soviet Union had collapsed and it seemed that socialism was dead as well. Even communist countries like China seemed to take up capitalism and abandon the idea of equality and social justice.

Socialists thought gradualism would work because the working class was the biggest group in society. It failed when most people became middle class and capitalism seemed to be able to work and improve living standards, while socialism seemed to fail, especially in the communist countries.

This is an example of an unbalanced answer. It deals with the 'why' about belief briefly in the introduction, the first sentence of the first paragraph, and again in the conclusion. The introduction makes a brief comment on 'why' and then describes how gradualism will happen. The candidate should have explained 'why' at greater length.

The first paragraph indicates that the candidate knows what gradualism meant in practice, but then drops into a largely descriptive approach, which is a common mistake. There is a description of gradual change, but no attempt to explain why the gradual changes were made. None of the statements in the answer are wrong but they are not explained and too disjointed to gain high marks.

This descriptive approach is the reason that the statements regarding why gradualism failed are not fully developed or connected. The answer to this question has to be focused on the 'why' aspect for both the belief and failure parts of the question. The last paragraph does introduce relevant contemporary international examples, but the implications of these are not explored.

The conclusion amounts to a brief statement of the outcome, rather than an evaluation of the arguments.

Marks
AO1 = 7
AO2 = 6 + 6 (for synopticity)
AO3 = 5
Total = 24

Anarchism

To what extent do anarchists agree about the nature of the future stateless society?

(45 marks)

> A comprehensive answer to this question requires a discussion of all aspects of the anarchist tradition. This means referring to not only the individual and collectivist views, but also to the different interpretations within each of these, such as libertarianism, anarcho-capitalism, mutualism, anarcho-communism and anarcho-syndicalism.

■ ■ ■

A-grade answer

Anarchists agree that there should be no state because it restricts and changes human nature from being peaceful and kind into being acquisitive and violent. Anarchists agree that there will be a natural order, no authority (religious or state) and a free market. However, there is a clear divide between individualist and collectivist anarchists with regard to the social arrangements and the economy and how it should be run.

Anarchists are united in their belief that natural order will arise in a future state-less society. This stems from their Utopian view of human nature, which argues that people cannot flourish under a state and will only reach their full, peaceful, potential when they are free from the state and religious authority and power. Faure defined anarchism as the 'negation of the principle of authority'.

The free market is the most desirable type of economy to have because it is the most efficient and is self-regulating without the interference of the state. However, the way the economy should go has caused the greatest divide between the two anarchist traditions, and will be discussed later.

Individualist anarchism, also known as ultra-liberalism, endorses an extreme form of individualism as the best arrangement for society. Classical liberals argued that individuals should be given negative freedom to do as they please. Individualist anarchists endorse this but without the confines of a state. This can be seen with the idea of egoism which is solely about the self. It was endorsed by Max Stirner, who argued that the individual should be left alone completely unless he or she wants to interact with others. This belief also suggests that individuals should be able to act how they please without following any moral rules. Society, for individualist anarchists, does not exist.

Collectivist anarchists reject this idea. They argue that the natural relationship between people is one of 'mutual aid' (Kropotkin) and cooperation. This is a form of ultra-socialism and endorses the use of communes as a way of organising society. Each commune would have a form of direct democracy where everyone had a say in everyday life. There would be no authority and no inequalities.

The economy divides anarchists even more. Individualist anarchists, influenced by Warren and Tucker, subscribe to a form of capitalism whereby there is a free market and free trade. Every individual is entitled to private property and can do with it what he or she pleases. Anarcho-capitalism is also characterised by a belief that it will regulate society because private companies will be set up to deal with disputes over contracts. Thus individualist anarchists subscribe to a completely unregulated market with complete privatisations. This will, they argue, lead to a more efficient service, and expand the ideals of individualism.

Collectivist anarchists completely oppose this individualist belief in a free market geared towards the benefit of the individual. Their socialist roots cause them to argue for a system of anarcho-communism, whereby the community works together by exchanging one product for another. There is no profit in an anarcho-communist society, in contrast with the individualist aim. Collectivist anarchists do not consider the privatisation of services because it will lead to the pursuit of profit, which they deplore because it creates inequalities. They want complete equality because only then will no hierarchy of authority exist.

All anarchists agree that a future stateless society will be peaceful and cooperative. However, individualist anarchists believe that it will be thus because of extreme individualism, libertarianism and anarcho-capitalism. Collectivist anarchists, on the other hand, believe that it will be peaceful because of mutual aid and anarcho-communism.

This is essay is an example of the necessity for good planning. The candidate is clearly able, using a number of sophisticated points, with appropriate references to individuals. However, the initial confusion with regard to attitudes to the free market means that the time and space spent over the error makes the second part of the answer on collectivist anarchism less sophisticated and not as well developed as the section on individualist anarchism. Failing to develop the points about the self-government of communities leads the candidate to completely omit anarcho-syndicalism, which has a clear view of a society based on trade unions.

One paragraph would have been sufficient to cover these points. This demonstrates how close the line can be between different levels of achievement.

The introduction sets up a comprehensive answer by dealing with the common ground and indicating areas of difference. However, it expresses confused opinions on the free market. It is followed by a clear and succinct anarchist view of the state, at which point the candidate remembers that there are differences over the free market.

There follows a good summary of the individualist position, with an appropriate reference to an individual thinker and a clear summary of the individualist position on the free market, again with a relevant reference to individual thinkers. The

answer concludes with an explanation of the 'collectivist' position and mentions anarcho-communism, but omits the other collectivist interpretation of anarcho-syndicalism.

The conclusion provides a succinct, if brief, summary of the different positions within anarchism that were asked for by the question.

Marks
AO1 = 9
AO2 = 10 + 10 (for synopticity)
AO3 = 8
Total = 37

■ ■ ■

C-grade answer

Anarchism is the belief in a society without a state. To anarchists, the state is an unnecessary evil which restricts the self-development of humans. In the argument of whether anarchism is closer to socialism or liberalism, it is necessary to define both socialism and liberalism in their various forms. Furthermore, because anarchism has never actually been successful in practice in modern society, we can only interpret its ideals through concepts developed by anarchist thinkers.

Socialism is the belief in the collectivisation of labour. Socialism, contrary to liberalism, believes in bringing people together. Liberalism, on the other hand, believes in the atomic nature of society, where the individual is foremost and at the centre of society.

Socialist thinkers such as Marx have had similar thoughts to anarchist thinkers. Socialism can be brought into practice in a number of ways. Firstly, socialism can arise through a revolution. This idea was envisaged by Marx. He believed that the proletariat, being suppressed for so long, would revolt and socialism would be created. Anarchists would not disagree, and to them a revolution might be a viable means to bring anarchy into practice. The second way of developing socialism would be through parliamentary means, where socialists would gain support through the ballot box. Anarchists here would disagree. They would argue that any means of state control or political activism is against the core principles of anarchism, the idea of a stateless society.

Liberalism is also similar to anarchism in a number of ways. Classical liberals advocate a belief in individualism. This is where the individual is at the centre and where individuals make decisions according to what they think is best. These ideas are similar to anarchism. Modern liberalism is different, there is a greater amount of state control and interference in the lives of individuals. Anarchists disagree with this.

Collectivisation and mutualism are at the centre of some anarchists thought. Collectivisation is the idea that people should work together without conflict and control. This is similar to the ideas of socialism. Mutualism was an idea developed by Kropotkin. It is the idea that people should exchange goods without seeking profit. This also is similar to socialism in that it promotes equality.

Anarcho-capitalism is a type of anarchist thought that agrees with capitalism. Capitalism is the free trade of goods and gives individuals the ability to create wealth. Anarcho-capitalism promotes this but on the basis of no government intervention. This shows a major link with liberal ideology.

Anarcho-syndicalism is a form of extreme trade unionism which was developed in France. Anarcho-syndicalists believe in direct action and sometimes even terrorism to ensure that they are not exploited. This is similar to socialism as it takes into account workers and promotes trade unions.

Anarchism promotes freedom of the individual so that people can roam freely without rules or restrictions. Most anarchists hold a positive view on human nature, the idea that humans are good and will become organised, sociable beings without government intervention. This view is held by both liberalism and socialism. Anarchism is also against organised religion, as religious belief tends to work hand in hand with political power. Therefore most anarchists believe in atheism. Liberalism, on the other hand, may advocate worship but with no restrictions on religion. Socialists would be against religion to an extent as religion creates tension within society. This shows that socialism and liberalism hold similar views to anarchism.

In conclusion, both socialism and liberalism have influenced anarchist thought. It is hard to identify whether anarchism is closer to one or the other. Different strands hold different views. Some of these agree with liberalism (anarcho-capitalism: freedom of the individual) and others with socialism (anarcho-syndicalism: mutualism and collectivism). It is therefore hard to identify whether anarchism as a whole is closer to liberalism or socialism.

🅔 This is an example of a candidate answering a different question to that which has been asked. This may happen because of misunderstanding the question or having revised an answer to a slightly different question. By answering a related question (about anarchism's relationship to socialism and liberalism), the candidate haphazardly makes creditworthy points at various stages through the essay, especially in the second half.

The introduction indicates that the candidate is preparing to answer a question that is different to the one asked: one about the relationship of anarchism to other ideologies.

The following paragraphs are not properly focused or sustained because of the consistent attempt to link anarchism with socialism or liberalism. It becomes stronger in the second half, when discussing anarcho-syndicalism,

question

anarcho-capitalism and the relationship of anarchism with individualism. All of these points are relevant to the question that has been asked. The conclusion, which sums up the disjointed nature of the answer as a whole, does not manage to go beyond the most basic statement of the anarchist position.

Marks
AO1 = 7
AO2 = 6 + 6 (for synopticity)
AO3 = 5
Total = 24